LOVE UNDOCUMENTED

"*Love Undocumented* is a wonderful story that will capture your imagination. Sarah Quezada is a gifted storyteller who has us laughing one minute, crying the next, and then wincing from punch-in-the-gut analysis. You will be delighted by the story and convicted by the message."

—LEROY BARBER, EXECUTIVE DIRECTOR OF THE VOICES PROJECT

"In *Love Undocumented*, Sarah Quezada peels back the curtain on complex immigration issues and those trapped within them. At a time when division reigns, Sarah offers an invitation to walk in solidarity and kinship with our immigrant neighbor."

—SHANNAN MARTIN, AUTHOR OF *FALLING FREE*

"Not many topics are more charged in today's world than the topic of immigration—not just in the larger culture but also in the church. In this climate, Sarah Quezada has written *Love Undocumented*: a poignant, honest, and nuanced account of her journey into the complex but real stories of immigration. This is a book that invites you into the story and, ultimately, into the heart of God. Stop shouting for a moment and read this book!"

—EUGENE CHO, SENIOR PASTOR OF QUEST CHURCH AND AUTHOR OF *OVERRATED*

"*Love Undocumented* powerfully walks us through the tragedy and triumph of the immigrant saga. Beyond facile or partisan platitudes, Sarah Quezada's story is a masterful and moving invitation to love our neighbors and to the power of human solidarity. Having read it, you will become richer."

—JEANETTE SALGUERO, SENIOR VICE PRESIDENT OF NATIONAL LATINO EVANGELICAL COALITION

"I am so grateful for Sarah Quezada's book and the way her story helps us to enter into the trauma that millions of undocumented men and women experience, trapped in our nation's broken immigration system. This book is a gift to every Christ-follower who is struggling to understand this complex issue from the vantage point of our faith."

—NOEL CASTELLANOS, PRESIDENT OF CHRISTIAN COMMUNITY DEVELOPMENT ASSOCIATION

"Honest and vulnerable, *Love Undocumented* is an invaluable resource for introducing and adding to our collective knowledge on the U.S. immigration system and how Christians should think about and engage it."

—KEN WYTSMA, AUTHOR OF *THE MYTH OF EQUALITY* AND FOUNDER OF THE JUSTICE CONFERENCE

"In *Love Undocumented*, Sarah Quezada has given us a much-needed narrative combined with great knowledge of the issues surrounding immigration. Blending story and factual data, Quezada places humanity back into this heated debate of immigration. I highly recommend this book."

—DANIEL WHITE HODGE, ASSOCIATE PROFESSOR OF YOUTH MINISTRY AT NORTH PARK UNIVERSITY AND AUTHOR OF *HOMELAND INSECURITY* AND *HIP HOP'S HOSTILE GOSPEL*

"I have not anticipated a book as much as I have *Love Undocumented*. Within these pages, you'll meet Sarah Quezada, a leader whose passion for bridge-building is evident in every story, every fact, every call to action. Both winsome and wise, this is the book we need right now."

—OSHETA MOORE, AUTHOR OF *SHALOM SISTAS*

"Sarah Quezada invites us into the complex world of U.S. immigration laws through her life experience and through a solid biblical and theological interpretation of God's love and care for foreigners and migrants. Quezada's challenge to trust God and immigrants is particularly timely."

—JUAN FRANCISCO MARTÍNEZ, PROFESSOR OF HISPANIC STUDIES AND PASTORAL LEADERSHIP AT FULLER THEOLOGICAL SEMINARY

"*Love Undocumented* is a poignant and highly revealing account of a journey into the perplexing, ethically conflicted, heartrending world of undocumented immigrants. A winsome and convicting work."

—BOB LUPTON, AUTHOR OF *TOXIC CHARITY* AND FOUNDER OF FCS URBAN MINISTRIES

"Immigration is a hot-button topic but one that is rarely addressed in thoughtful, nuanced, dignifying ways by the people who are most affected by this issue. I have been waiting impatiently for *Love Undocumented* to be published so I could give it to everyone I know."

—D. L. MAYFIELD, AUTHOR OF *ASSIMILATE OR GO HOME*

"*Love Undocumented* will have you alternating between laughter and tears. Both personal and profound, this deftly written book will both entertain you and move you closer to God's heart for the immigrant."

—MATTHEW SOERENS, COAUTHOR OF *SEEKING REFUGE* AND *WELCOMING THE STRANGER* AND U.S. CHURCH TRAINING SPECIALIST FOR WORLD RELIEF

"Sarah Quezada has written a masterpiece. Quezada dives into the biblical basis for our concern for immigrants, reminding us that we have a God of radical hospitality and liberation and that we worship a Savior who was a displaced Galilean. But perhaps the most important thing Quezada does is make this 'issue' personal. Quezada puts a name and face on who our neighbor really is."

—SHANE CLAIBORNE, SPEAKER, AUTHOR, AND ACTIVIST

"*Love Undocumented* is a beautifully written book about what happens when a political issue becomes intimately personal. Sarah Quezada reminds us that immigration involves real people with real stories and that everything changes when we enter into deep relationships with them."

—SHAWN CASSELBERRY, EXECUTIVE DIRECTOR OF MISSION YEAR AND COAUTHOR OF *SOUL FORCE*

"If you believe that you should love your neighbor, read this book. Sarah Quezada has a life story of living love and will give you the chance to see a greater view of your neighbor in today's world."

—JEFF SHINABARGER, FOUNDER OF PLYWOOD PEOPLE AND AUTHOR OF *MORE OR LESS*

"At Casa Alterna, our motto is 'Love crosses borders.' After years of friendship with Sarah and Billy Quezada, I have witnessed this to be true of their marriage. *Love Undocumented* is a hopeful gift to a world tempted to build walls of fear and mistrust."

—ANTON FLORES-MAISONET, COFOUNDER OF CASA ALTERNA AND EL REFUGIO

"Weaving personal story, biblical principles, and informed facts around immigration, *Love Undocumented* gives voice to the injustice facing undocumented immigrants and their families, further compelling us to move beyond our fear toward building transforming relationships."

—MICHELLE WARREN, ADVOCACY AND STRATEGIC ENGAGEMENT DIRECTOR OF THE CHRISTIAN COMMUNITY DEVELOPMENT ASSOCIATION AND AUTHOR OF THE *POWER OF PROXIMITY*

"*Love Undocumented* is a journal of accompaniment into the confusing labyrinth that is the life of undocumented immigrants. We need books like this to remind us that migration is about people, about family, about life together."

—M. DANIEL CARROLL R., AUTHOR OF *CHRISTIANS AT THE BORDER* AND BLANCHARD PROFESSOR OF OLD TESTAMENT AT WHEATON COLLEGE

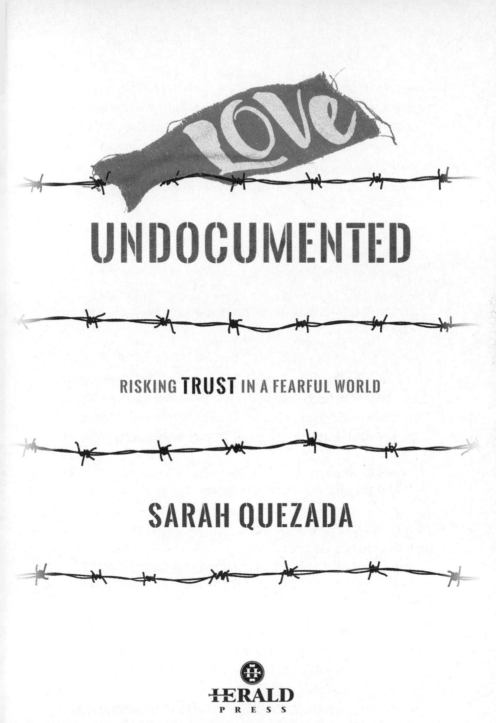

LOVE

UNDOCUMENTED

RISKING **TRUST** IN A FEARFUL WORLD

SARAH QUEZADA

HERALD
P R E S S

Harrisonburg, Virginia

Herald Press
PO Box 866, Harrisonburg, Virginia 22803
www.HeraldPress.com

Library of Congress Cataloging-in-Publication Data
Names: Quezada, Sarah, author.
Title: Love undocumented : risking trust in a fearful world / Sarah Quezada.
Description: Harrisonburg : Herald Press, 2018. | Includes bibliographical
    references.
Identifiers: LCCN 2017043593| ISBN 9781513803074 (pbk. : alk. paper) | ISBN
    9781513803081 (hardcover : alk. paper)
Subjects: LCSH: Church work with immigrants. | Emigration and
    immigration--Religious aspects--Christianity.
Classification: LCC BV639.I4 Q49 2018 | DDC 261.8/36--dc23 LC record
    available at https://lccn.loc.gov/2017043593

Unless otherwise noted, Scripture quotations are from the ESV® Bible (*The Holy Bible, English Standard Version®*), copyright © 2001 by Crossway, a publishing ministry of Good News Publishers. Used by permission. All rights reserved.

Scripture marked *The Message* is quoted with permission, copyright © 1993, 1994, 1995, 1996, 2000, 2001, 2002. Used by permission of NavPress Publishing Group.

Scripture marked (NLT) is taken from the Holy Bible, New Living Translation, copyright © 1996, 2004, 2007 by Tyndale House Foundation. Used by permission of Tyndale House Publishers, Inc., Carol Stream, Illinois 60188. All rights reserved.

Sections of chapter 10 are adapted from an article originally published on ChristianityToday.com titled "My Marriage to an Undocumented Immigrant." Portions of chapter 12 appeared as a December 16, 2016, blog post at Gracetable.org. Portions of chapter 13 first appeared as "Kindness Versus Quotas," in *Geez*, Winter 2016. Sections of chapter 13 are adapted from an article originally published on ChristianityToday .com titled "I Saw Jesus in Detention." Sections of chapters 3 and 11 are adapted from an article originally published on ChristianityToday.com titled "How Churches Can Give Sanctuary and Still Support the Law."

LOVE UNDOCUMENTED
© 2018 by Herald Press, Harrisonburg, Virginia 22803. 800-245-7894.
All rights reserved.
Library of Congress Control Number: 2017043593
International Standard Book Number: 978-1-5138-0307-4 (paperback);
    978-1-5138-0308-1 (hardcover); 978-1-5138-0309-8 (ebook)
Printed in United States of America
Cover and interior design by Merrill Miller
Photo on p. 79 by Irinoa Juarez. Photo on p. 150 by Ryan Secrest. Photo on p. 167 by
    Lydia Phillips and used by permission of El Refugio. Other photos courtesy of the
    author.

22 21 20 19 18   10 9 8 7 6 5 4 3 2 1

For Billy

CONTENTS

FOREWORD

Three things will last forever—faith, hope, and love—and the greatest of these is love. —1 Corinthians 13:13 NLT

Love Undocumented is a rich resource for anyone seeking to understand our immigration crisis; it is full of information and inspiration. First and foremost, however, it is a compelling love story.

Love is the most powerful motivation I know. Of course, we know that fear and anger have a major impact on our society, in both intimate and public arenas. I have watched, over the past thirty years, the ways in which fear and anger have contributed to the increasing brokenness of our immigration system. I have seen all the damage that fear and anger have wreaked on the families in our church. There have been detailed bipartisan legislative proposals to create a system that would be effective, fair, and humane. They have failed, but not because of the opposition of the American people; each proposal has polled at over 70 percent support. The most recent proposal passed the Senate in 2013. Advocates of immigration reform knew that we would have had enough Republican and Democratic votes to pass the bill in the House of Representatives. But it was never brought to the floor of the House for a vote. Our leaders do not consider immigration an important enough issue on which to take a risk.

This beautiful book opens the heart and feeds the mind. Sarah Quezada's personal love story is woven seamlessly with a comprehensive, accurate picture of the workings of our current immigration system and its impact on our communities. I cried my way through this book as I remembered so many similar experiences. Having also married an immigrant from Latin America, I am familiar both with the ridiculous and horrible experiences Quezada describes and with the beauty of God's Spirit at work in the midst of the pain.

Please get this book for anyone you know who does not know from personal experience how and why people are suffering unjustly in our neighborhoods. *Love Undocumented* is particularly important for Christian believers. There is only one institution in our society that is mandated to care passionately about people who are not "us": the church. The more that non-immigrants step up to partner with immigrants, the more we see the exchange of hope and passion that can fuel sustained work for change. Immigrants who have lost hope find their hope restored through allies; nonimmigrants discover a new level of passion for change as they fall in love with those who are on the front lines of the crisis.

If every believer read *Love Undocumented*, the Spirit of God might move through our churches like a mighty wind and, in the words of Ephesians 2, break down the dividing walls that keep immigrant and nonimmigrant believers apart. John 17:21 reminds us that the world knows that Jesus has come by the unity of his followers. The world does not know Jesus has come just because Baptists and Methodists work together. The world knows that Jesus has come when Christ-followers take risks to stand courageously with immigrants. May *Love Undocumented* be the spark for that witness to occur.

—*Alexia Salvatierra, Lutheran pastor, founder of the Faith-Rooted Organizing Network, and coauthor of* Faith-Rooted Organizing

AUTHOR'S NOTE

Thank you for picking up this book. I'm excited to walk together through the U.S. immigration system in these pages. It's a personal journey for me and for so many families in our country, and it's an honor to share with you.

My hope is always to treat others with dignity, including the language I choose. In this book, you will see the word *illegal* used to describe actions but not people (with some limited exceptions in dialogue). Though not perfect, descriptors like *undocumented* or *unauthorized* will be used when needed for clarity and distinction.

While we will explore many different facets of immigration, *Love Undocumented* is not an exhaustive resource on the topic. To give you an idea of what that might look like, the eighteenth edition of the book *U.S. Immigration Made Easy* is 688 pages long. I have a feeling its author would say there's more to unpack as well.

This book chronicles my personal experience and should not be used as a guide for your own legal process. My best legal advice is to hire a reputable immigration attorney. (If you need one, I know a guy.) Laws are changing rapidly, and it's important to be adequately informed about your specific situation.

Finally, the narrative portions of this book are my own recollections of the events as I experienced them. Some names have been changed for clarity or privacy. I do my best to stay true to the heart of the story, but I'm sure my memories have gaps and blips that I will lovingly blame on my children.

Thanks again for reading, and let's jump in!

—*Sarah Quezada*

STAIRWELLS AND BUNKERS

a small bell chirped as the ice cream vendor pushed through the crowded sidewalk. Colorful stickers slapped on the sides of the cart advertised ice cream sandwiches, rainbow popsicles, chocolate-dipped concoctions rolled in nuts. Impeded by the crowds, he bumped over the curb and into the street, pushing his cart faster and hollering "¡Helado!" (Ice cream!) to the parents and children teeming up and down each side of the busy street. Loud, tempting sizzles cracked in the air as street vendors fried hot dogs wrapped in bacon. Norteño music blared from the park on one side of the sidewalk and Spanish pop flowed from storefront *pupuserías* (Salvadoran restaurants) across the street. Bass beats boomed from cars waiting at traffic lights, and mothers pushed strollers and held tightly to toddlers while crossing the intersection.

I tried not to gawk. The day before, I had driven my Nissan Sentra, crammed with all my personal belongings, into downtown Los Angeles. My dear friend Jennifer had spent the last week driving with me from Kentucky—more than two thousand miles across the country—to help me get settled into my new place before she flew back home a few days later. We had lived together for the last two years while I attended graduate school. After graduation, I had accepted a job at an L.A.-area Christian university to help lead an urban studies program. It was my dream job, so I'd packed up and gone west even though I knew no one, nor had any idea what I was getting into.

Our plan had been to walk from my new apartment to the nearest subway station, which I could take to get to my office. But we were not entirely sure we were heading in the right direction, so we instead allowed the swell and flow of people to push us along. I felt jostled from every side. Teenagers bumped me as they passed. Families squeezed together so pedestrians could form makeshift "lanes" on the narrow sidewalk. Men leaning against buildings on the corners of alleyways whispered "Psst!" to catch my eye and offer "ID? ID?" while rubbing their fingers together. They looked at me imploringly. I had no idea what was happening. Still, I resisted the urge to pull the neatly folded Los Angeles map out of my back pocket, where I'd hidden it to avoid looking like a tourist.

But I'd never felt more like an outsider. My travel experience was limited, and I had been outside of the United States exactly three times, two of those to Canada when I worked as a summer camp counselor in Vermont and chaperoned kids to Canadian attractions. The other time was a visit to the Los Angeles exurbs with some friends when we decided to "go to Mexico for lunch." We made no plan and consulted no map. We figured if we got turned around, we just needed to ask "¿Dónde está la playa?" (Where is the beach?) and then turn right. Clearly the well-thought-out itinerary of savvy international travelers.

But as Jennifer and I walked toward what I hoped would be the Westlake/MacArthur Park subway station, I felt as if I had left the States once again. Spanish floated through the air and adorned business signs, no one I saw looked like me, and the pedestrian crowds were overwhelming. In fact, the area was the second most dense neighborhood in Los Angeles, with more than 38,000 people per square mile.[1] It was also a heavily immigrant community, boasting a high percentage of foreign-born people even for L.A. Approximately 90 percent of residents were Latino or Asian, and Mexico and El Salvador were the most common countries of foreign birth.[2]

I may have come to Los Angeles to guide college students through an urban semester program, but I was woefully unprepared for this expression of America.

* * *

The changing face of the country has dominated the political discourse, as well as dinner table conversations, off and on throughout U.S. history. The topic of immigration has flared again, with particular attention to undocumented arrivals from south of the border, as well as the surging refugee population from war-plagued countries like Syria. According to the Migration Policy Institute, in 2015 around 13.5 percent of the U.S. population, or 43.3 million people, were immigrants.[3] And immigrants have continued to move, whether legally or illegally, into communities throughout the country.

These new arrivals make an impact in their local neighborhoods, and longtime residents have mixed reactions. As well-known journalist and Spanish-language news anchor Jorge Ramos said in an interview, "There's no question that we are in the middle of a demographic revolution that is affecting everything, from the way we eat, to the way we dance, to the way we vote. . . . This trend has created two very different reactions. On one hand, millions of Americans embracing immigrants and embracing foreigners and embracing the changes, and a few other millions rejecting that change."[4]

Many of us have witnessed the fear and distrust of immigrants and refugees grow, especially as new arrivals have been saddled with the weight of all social ills. Drugs, violence, unemployment, gangs, rape, terrorism, secularism, and more are fashioned into a narrative that scapegoats some of the world's most exploited and vulnerable peoples.

But while some politicians prey on fears of the Other, many people, including Christians, feel uncertain about what is really going on with immigrants. Is it true that unchecked masses are pouring over our borders? Why aren't people just following the proper procedures? What does reasonable and compassionate engagement look like? In my interview for the Los Angeles position, I had been told my job would include working closely with immigrant families. I was enthusiastic about this prospect, although I admitted in the conversation that I knew almost nothing about the political "sides" regarding the topic. In an effort to assure the interviewer I could serve families in this capacity, I mumbled something about liking to meet new people and generally favoring that others feel welcomed in this country.

That halfhearted answer pretty much summed up my entire "opinion" on immigration. Heated political debates and sensational statistics just didn't resonate with me. I know I'm not alone in preferring to avoid these fiery approaches to the topic. Conversations about immigration can feel exhausting, and they are often divorced from the real people hiding behind the speeches and the numbers. So much nuance is lost in the binary perspectives of liberal versus conservative, Republican versus Democrat, or Left versus Right.

But I believe Christians want to engage immigrants in their communities—as well as the national immigration conversation—in ways that uphold the Bible and honor the dignity of people from all over the world.

Unfortunately, few churches are having conversations about immigration. A 2015 study from LifeWay Research revealed only one in five evangelical Christians said their local church had ever encouraged them to reach out to immigrants in their communities. Yet almost 70 percent of those surveyed said they would appreciate a sermon that taught how biblical principles and examples could be applied to the issue of immigration.[5]

Navigating the vehement tones of the current immigration debate can be unsettling. How do we resist the political fear-mongering? How do we balance our desire to love our neighbor with real questions and concerns about the ways immigration affects us? How do we talk with sisters and brothers in the church about what has become a "political" question—even and perhaps especially if we disagree?

As I flowed with the crowd along the buzzing, swirling street, I felt completely overwhelmed. I grabbed Jennifer's arm and pulled her into a small staircase descending from the street. A low wall shielded us from the pulsing sidewalks. I sat down and took a breath. I was surrounded by strangers, people I didn't know from places I'd never seen, speaking a language I'd barely learned in college.

Growing up, my generation was warned about "stranger danger"—the idea that someone unknown might very well be a threat. The best way to handle a situation with unfamiliar persons was to flee, to run and tell a grown-up, to find safety. Under no circumstances should you escalate the interaction by speaking to a stranger, accepting their candy, or climbing into their windowless van. Unfortunately, I never revisited this childhood strategy, or developed a more robust and mature approach to encountering the stranger. I'm not sure my friends or other Christians I knew had either.

Are we taught how to thoughtfully engage with people who are unfamiliar? As Christians, do we really grapple with how Scripture instructs us to welcome the stranger? In *The Irresistible Revolution*, author Shane Claiborne writes, "I had come to see that the great tragedy of the church is not that rich Christians do not care about the poor but that rich Christians do not know the poor."[6] This sentiment rings exceedingly true when we talk about immigration. Barriers like language, religion, and cultural customs—not to mention the fact that communities are segregated by race and class—make relationships between native-born citizens and immigrants challenging. Many of us born in the United States simply do not know immigrants. It's especially unlikely that we have relationships with those who are undocumented and living in the shadows of mainstream society. That isolation certainly described my own situation when I pulled into Los Angeles as a young adult.

Lack of relationship is a breeding ground for fear. Fear and anxiety pervade the conversation about immigrants and refugees. Indeed, these feelings seem to have taken up permanent residence in the American psyche. In a 2016 article for *Curbed*, journalist Patrick Sisson spoke with contractors and security firms specializing in high-end fortified panic rooms and bunkers. While privacy concerns prevented these companies from sharing specific numbers or details about clients, Sisson reported that everyone interviewed for the piece testified they'd seen business growth in the last decade.[7] These modern-day luxury clients are hiring professionals to construct bulletproof family rooms, bomb-safe bedrooms, and underground bunkers complete with swimming pools, exercise rooms, and shooting ranges.

Of course, some protective structures, particularly storm shelters, have always been a part of some Americans' lives. "Built with neighbors," Sisson notes, "they were a symbol of a new settlement and an expanded community." But then Sisson makes a very startling distinction: "Today, shelters and bunkers are an escape from community, motivated by a belief that our society is fraying and unable to cope with coming civil unrest, terrorism, or other destabilizing events."[8] Fear is escalating isolation, which yields even more insecurity and uncertainty.

* * *

Jennifer and I hid out in our own staircase bunker and spread the map over our legs. I gingerly traced the roads from my new apartment, peeking out from behind the wall to read street signs. My finger landed on my current position in the Westlake/MacArthur Park community, a mere block from my destination subway station. I felt a tiny spring of tears at the corner of my eyes. We had not taken a wrong turn. In fact, we were right on track. This chaotic and noisy walk was my new commute to work. I felt unsure of myself. I felt overwhelmed. I felt a little afraid. And my reaction surprised me.

My penchant for new experiences, as well as my faith background, had merged into a foundational belief that fear, while an acceptable emotion, was not something on which to dwell or on which to make decisions. I'd grown up memorizing Bible verses with G.T. and the Halo Express. From one of their songs, I discovered my favorite Scripture, Isaiah 41:10: "Fear not, for I am with you; be not dismayed, for I am your God; I will strengthen you, I will help you, I will uphold you with my righteous right hand." I had never assumed that the Christian life would come without uncertainty or suffering, but I was relatively confident that God would be present in any unfamiliar circumstances.

I also took great comfort in the many Scriptures in which the people of God are reminded not to be afraid. Over and over, when God bursts onto the scene, the first command is to "fear not." When God shows up in a vision to Abram, the initial dialogue in Genesis 15:1 is "Fear not, Abram, I am your shield; your reward shall be very great." Then God proceeds to make a covenant with him. When Gabriel visits Mary to tell her she's carrying the Christ child, she is confused by his greeting. He immediately responds, "Do not be afraid, Mary, for you have found favor with God" (Luke 1:30). Similarly, the shepherds are surprised by an angel of the Lord, who leads with "Fear not, for behold, I bring you good news of great joy that will be for all the people" (Luke 2:10). When Jesus overhears others telling Jairus that his daughter has died, Jesus interjects himself into the conversation, saying, "Do not fear, only believe" (Mark 5:36), before he heads to Jairus's house to raise his daughter from the dead. Hagar, Joshua, the disciples who see Jesus walk on water: all these people of God and more are reassured that, though they are encountering the unfamiliar, the audacious, the overwhelming, they don't need to be afraid.

* * *

So how do we welcome strangers in a world that defaults to fear? When the divine breaks into our day-to-day lives, will we panic and miss God's presence? To avoid the isolation that cultivates fear of the Other, we have a pressing need for community. Relationships across cultural barriers are an antidote to fear. The distant, mythical immigrant "out there" is much more intimidating and menacing than, say, the immigrant mom at preschool pickup who is trying to convince her own stubborn toddler that leaving the playground and going home to take a nap is a great idea. When presented with risk and fear of the unknown, we have the opportunity to choose our response. We can be wary or be welcoming.

When Sisson interviewed the founder of Black Umbrella, a safety business that helps families prepare for disasters, she made a similar observation about the ways Americans are reacting to life's threats.

> It would be my personal preference that people confront these security issues by becoming more a part of the community, better at tribe building, and more resilient. The trend appears to be heading towards social isolation and pessimism, to build an island in my house and close the door. It's great to have in your back pocket, but it doesn't replace everyday situational awareness. I don't want to critique other Americans, but it's like the difference between working out and plastic surgery. Both things will get you where you want to be, but one thing will leave you more prepared. I would love to see our country do more of the hard work.[9]

Community building in an age of fear: what a beautiful and countercultural opportunity for the church. What would it look like if we took the lead in stepping out across the lines of fear and uncertainty? What if Christians began to see relationships as central to repairing a broken social fabric and worked together for compassionate change? We are not called to fear and isolation. The thread of Scripture draws us over and over again into relationship with God and relationship with others, all the while reminding us not to be afraid.

Love Undocumented recounts my story of risking trust in a fearful world. Join me as I meet new people and experience unexpected situations. Both during these real-life events and in the telling of them here, I have been constantly learning and asking new questions. I have been surprised by the appearance of God in the face of the Other, and I have marveled at the ways that God has nudged and tugged me out of fear and into trust. I hope you will find the same.

Sitting on those concrete steps, listening to the accordion music floating through the air, I didn't yet know that the invitation to welcome the stranger is an open door to abundant life filled with cake, dance parties, and piñatas. I had no idea that I would soon meet a handsome stranger from Guatemala, or that he would lead me into a hidden world of experiences I'd never known—from construction sites to Central America to lawyer's offices and back again.

All I knew was that this diverse, bustling city was my new home, and I needed to find my way. Jennifer and I stood up and ascended the stairs. Pressing back into the streaming crowds, we headed toward the subway station.

2

COFFEE WITH A ROCK STAR

*H*i Sarah. This is Billy. Would you like to grav some coffee Saturday?"

I read the text message while lying in a tent near the beach. A month into my second semester working at the university, I was leading an overnight camping retreat for my students. Everyone was off with a reading assignment and some quiet time for prayer.

I stared at the text. "Hi Sarah. This is Billy."

Billy and I had met the previous weekend at my church when he'd walked up and started talking to me after the service. Feeling disoriented by his demeanor of familiarity, I'd stuck out my hand and offered what I thought was a friendly "Hi! I don't think we've met before."

But he'd only taken my hand and smiled. "Yes, Sarah, we have. Twice, actually."

I froze in embarrassment. I may have been living in California, but I was a southern girl at heart. Given my firmly rooted ideas about politeness and good manners, I was horrified. Forgetting ever meeting someone was not the southern way. I faltered. "Um . . . oh. I'm sorry. I don't remember your name."

A couple of hours later, we'd ended up going to see a movie with some mutual friends, who were also a married couple. I was still convinced that this activity hadn't been as "accidental" as everyone was making it out to be. But I had to admit, I'd was intrigued by Billy. He was cute, with short hair and brown eyes and just enough scruff that he didn't look too clean-cut. I found his accent endearing, though it had surprised me when he'd first spoken. Later, he'd told me that he had emigrated from Guatemala. Our small talk had been easy, and he'd seemed genuinely interested to learn about my family and my home in Kentucky.

Still, I found myself hesitating about seeing him again. "Would you like to grav some coffee Saturday?" Trying not to focus on the spelling error—and not knowing that the *b* and *v* sounds in Spanish are almost identical—I was skeptical that he and I would have much in common. After all, he was from a different country, and I didn't even have a passport. Not to mention we didn't speak the same first language, which I imagined would make real communication nearly impossible. But he had been friendly and interesting, I thought, so what could a coffee date hurt?

I texted back. "Sounds great. How's 2?"

* * *

Most of us spend our time and form our relationships with people who are like us. Our communities are largely segregated by race and class, and we tend to gravitate toward those who have similar levels of education, work in related fields, or share our general values and worldview. Churches, book clubs, and community organizations all help us form new relationships based on common interests. We assume that these friendships have a foundation already set in place and on which it will be easier to build a long-lasting relationship.

But our draw to what's most familiar means many of us do not have significant diverse friendships. In a 2014 article for the *Washington Post*, Christopher Ingraham analyzes data from the Public Religion Research Institute about the racial makeup of black and white Americans' core relationship networks. The institute found that "the average black person's friend network is 8 percent white, but the average white person's network is only 1 percent black." Ingraham puts it bluntly: "Blacks have ten times as many black friends as white friends. But white Americans have an astonishing 91 times as many white friends as black friends." It's sobering to note that for both white and black Americans, only 2 percent of their core relationships were with Latinos or Asians.[1] While immigrants may fall into any of these racial categories, the intensity of homogeneous networks makes it logical to assume most white and black Americans are not in close relationships with immigrants.

One of the ways Jesus constantly astonished and scandalized his followers was to cross over boundaries and build relationships across different backgrounds. In John 4, Jesus is on his way to Galilee and passes through Samaria. The Jews and the Samaritans were bitter enemies, but Jesus sits beside a local well and asks a Samaritan woman for a drink of water. They proceed to have a lively conversation about salvation, infidelity, and religious practices. When Jesus' disciples return, "they marveled that he was talking with a woman, but no one said, 'What do you seek?' or, 'Why are you talking with her?'" (John 4:27). I love that the disciples are freaked out but that no one has the courage to ask Jesus about it.

The disciples have no problem, however, trying to keep children away from Jesus. He is, after all, a big-deal preacher, teacher, and healer. But when parents bring their kids to Jesus for prayer, he says to his disciples, "Let the little children come to me and do not hinder them, for to such belongs the kingdom of heaven" (Matthew 19:14). In another example, Jesus invites himself to the home of Zacchaeus, a corrupt rich man, which causes the people to grumble (Luke 19:7).

Jesus connected across all of society's boundaries: gender, ethnicity and race, age, occupation, class, and religion. He lived an example of radical friendship that didn't seek out only those who shared his exact background and familiar characteristics. Instead, he looked for those working in the heat of the day, waiting in the wings to be blessed, and climbing into trees for a glimpse of God.

Jesus walked into history and started rubbing elbows with shepherds and tax collectors. Should he walk into today, I think we would find him talking with day laborers in the parking lot of a home improvement warehouse and inviting himself home to dinner with the CEOs of private prisons and detention centers. Relationships are the foundation for restoration and compassionate community, and Jesus reached across the human barriers that divide people.

* * *

We sat outside Starbucks, the late February warmth streaming onto our table. I sipped my vanilla latte as Billy described his work, which involved climbing on roofs to install satellite dishes. He asked about my position at the university and about my family.

My roommate and I were considering a summer trip to Guatemala to work on our Spanish. When I told Billy of our potential plans, he immediately warned me that the month of

May, which we'd chosen because of our work schedules, was the absolute worst time to visit thanks to the rainy season. I tried to explain that was the only time I could go, but he simply shrugged and encouraged me to go another time. I also told him I was reading a book about Guatemala's civil war, and Billy nodded. "It ended in 1996," he reminded me. "I grew up during it." Unsure how to respond to such an unfamiliar declaration, I mumbled something indiscernible before changing the topic.

"So why did you come to the States?" I asked him.

Billy answered casually, "Oh, I came to California to participate in a world singing competition." I started to laugh, but stopped short because I didn't want to be rude. Was he joking? I never expected that answer. I looked at his face, but I couldn't tell by his smile if he was serious or not.

"What on earth?" I exclaimed, with hands in the air. Then I badgered him with questions until he finally confessed: he was the former lead singer of a Christian hardcore band.

I burst into surprised laughter. Nothing about his relatively clean-cut appearance betrayed his passion for screaming into a microphone. I was intrigued.

It turned out he was a passionate drummer and guitar player, and yes, had also taken voice lessons to learn how to scream correctly into a microphone to achieve that perfect level of hardcore angst without damaging his vocal chords. His Guatemalan rock band had traveled all over Central America, visiting churches and performing before audiences that sang along to their hit song. "No More Suffer" had received decent radio play and even been covered by a Mexican band.

I set my latte down and inched forward in my seat, hands tucked under my chin. I had never expected this fantastical backstory! Hanging onto every detail, I found myself more and more charmed by Billy. I was pleasantly surprised how easily

Billy's headshot for a musical competition in Los Angeles.

the conversation flowed, how much I enjoyed his company, and how quickly he made me laugh.

We continued our conversation and shared about our experiences living in Los Angeles. For some reason I disclosed that I had yet to visit Rodeo Drive, a famous luxury shopping district. Billy was astounded by this "big reveal," especially because he was certain it wasn't that far from where we were sitting. I balked at this pronouncement.

"If you don't believe me, we can get in my Jeep right now and I will prove it to you." Billy's eyes twinkled. I toyed with my empty coffee cup.

"Fine," I declared, standing up from the table and simultaneously agreeing to extend this first date beyond coffee.

We climbed into his black Jeep and headed in the direction of Rodeo Drive. And it was exactly where he'd said it would be. As we walked along and peeked into the windows of the high-end shops, we talked about our faith backgrounds. Billy once again surprised me. He had been a youth pastor at a megachurch in Guatemala. In fact, he had been one of the early leaders in what had since become the biggest church in the country, with thousands in attendance each week.

I shared with him how I had grown up a young, southern evangelical in the late 1980s and early '90s. Christianity with a lot of rules was a comforting structure for my personality, since it helped me to know what was expected of me and if I was following through. But as I'd entered my young adult years, I found myself feeling antsy. I didn't mind keeping the rules, and I wasn't exactly craving rebellion. More than anything, I was bored.

Around the same time, I was also inexplicably drawn to the city. To the diversity, to the bustle, to the hype, to the crowds. In my context, the only real way to express this interest was by declaring an intent to become an urban missionary. So I did. I'm sure some friends and relatives thought the idea would wear off before I graduated from college. But I decided to take a year off after my freshman year to serve with Mission Year, a yearlong Christian volunteer program in the city.[2] During this immersive experience of living cross-culturally and building relationships with people from different backgrounds, my faith had come alive.

Through my neighbors in the city, I'd experienced God in new ways. I was invited to Thanksgiving dinner, where I ate collard greens flavored with ham hock while sitting on our hosts' bed with the TV on. In one of the poorest homes I'd ever seen, just a room really, I also sat on the bed while my neighbors offered me boiled pigs' feet with hot sauce, which I'd never eaten before; I washed it down with lukewarm Pepsi. These new experiences provided me tangible connection to the Bible story of the widow's mite when God rejoiced at the woman whose generosity and faith transcended her financial situation.

I interacted with women who slid into strangers' cars, leveraging their bodies for financial support and meeting their intertwined needs and addictions. As a woman walking through that neighborhood, I experienced the indignity of people making assumptions about my participation in these activities as well. And I thought about the woman at the well, who had known many men. Who had sinned and likely been exploited. I understood anew how shocking and provocative it was that Jesus sat with and spoke to this woman, and treated her with dignity and respect.

My first taste of living among the poor in the city had invigorated my faith, reshaped my future, and even contributed to my being hired at the California university. Now it was Billy's turn to be surprised. We were both turning out to be a little bit different than the other had presumed.

As the dinner hour neared, Billy tentatively asked if we wanted to eat. "Maybe at one of the restaurants here?" he offered, glancing around Rodeo Drive.

I wasn't ready for the date to end, but I also wasn't interested in a fancy meal. "Or we could get *pupusas*," I suggested.

"Pupusas?" He was stunned. "How do you know pupusas?" Before I moved to L.A., I'd never tasted the thick tortillas stuffed with fillings like beans and cheese and topped with coleslaw. But once I'd tried this signature food of El Salvador, Guatemala's neighbor, I was all in. "I don't even know where to get pupusas here!" Billy admitted.

"You know how to find Rodeo Drive with no problem," I chided, "but you're a Guatemalan who has no idea where to find pupusas?" I laughed. "I know a place."

From the passenger seat, I proceeded to direct him to MacArthur Park and the crowded neighborhood I'd stumbled into my first weekend in the city. Eight months had passed since then, and I had walked the streets many times and learned more about the neighborhood. I had heard the rumors about bodies in the bottom of the lake, and I'd finally understood that the men nodding their heads at me and rubbing their fingers together were part of the area's notorious illegal document trade. Social Security cards, birth certificates, driver's licenses, green cards, student IDs: you name it, someone in MacArthur Park could likely secure it for you. New identities could be purchased for around one hundred dollars.

But through my connections to immigrant families and service agencies in the neighborhood, I had also learned about some of the best hole-in the-wall eateries. Billy parked, and we walked up to a nondescript storefront. He looked only slightly concerned; the sun was starting to set and vendors were packing up their carts to head home. "Are you sure this is it?" he asked. "And we're good here?"

"Yep," I told him, as he grabbed the door to hold it open. I smiled to myself. The day had not turned out at all how I'd expected. And mostly, it was because Billy was not at all who I'd presumed him to be.

It would have been easy to allow a spelling error to confirm my suspicion that the gulf between us was too big to cross. But when we take a risk and step across societal divides, we may be pleasantly surprised by the connections and similarities we discover. Unlike the West's unrestrained exaltation of the individual, Scripture reminds us that we are all created in God's image (Genesis 1:27) and that God's overwhelming love for us precipitated Jesus' arrival to save us all (John 3:16). We are united by our shared humanity. Every person—with their cultural background, language, sense of humor, musical tastes, and more—gives us a wider view of who God is.

Unforeseen twists had led to a marathon first date—one that kept me guessing and wanting to know more. Little did I know that Billy was holding on to more startling information. But that wouldn't come until our third date.

3

ILLEGAL

A small child in a sequined unitard stood straight and rigid, perched on his father's hand held high in the air. The passers-by who had stopped to watch cheered for the little boy and tossed money into the duo's bucket on the ground. Billy and I walked past, enjoying the late afternoon along Third Street Promenade, a pedestrian-friendly shopping district in Santa Monica. He reached for my hand as we navigated around a group of tourists eating ice cream.

As we walked by mannequins in a store window, Billy said, "You know, when I came here to the States? I came for the contest. You remember?"

I laughed. "I will never forget!"

"Well, when I arrived, I came on a tourist visa," he continued.

"Cool," I responded, turning my head at the sound of tap shoes clickety-clacking on the other side of the street.

"Yeah." Billy coughed, and I looked back at him.

"Well, I have a ten-year visa," he said, and waited without making eye contact. I wasn't sure how to respond: Good for you? I wondered why he was telling me these details about his travel arrangements.

"But actually," he continued, "even though my visa is good for ten years, I'm not supposed to stay for more than six months at a time."

I wrinkled my forehead. I knew he'd been here for more than six months. He'd already told me he had come to the States almost two years before. "So . . ." I paused, unsure of what to say. "Is that a problem?"

"Well, it's a little tricky," Billy admitted. "I wish when I'd gotten near the six-month mark I would have gone down to Tijuana for the day. Then I would've left the country like my visa required and been able to return the next day, no problem."

"Why didn't you?"

"I don't know," he said. "I wasn't really paying attention. And I didn't think I'd be here that long, so it wasn't on my mind."

I had questions, but I wasn't certain what they were or how to ask. But I continued, "So how come you ended up staying longer than you thought?"

"Well, when I came, I had a girlfriend back in Guatemala. But we broke up while I was here, and I didn't want to go home to all of that. I had also had a company in Guatemala, but it hadn't worked out. So I started to feel like I didn't want to go back and live with my parents without a job."

I nodded, and he continued. "I had work here, so I just kept going. But I was at the job site most days of the week, and it was hard to take a day off and leave the country to deal with my visa. If I had it to do over, though, I would have made the time."

Billy paused. We walked along quietly for a while until he said, "Now I'm trying to see how I can work things out."

I wasn't completely sure what he was trying to tell me. What did he mean by "work things out"? Was this his halting way of telling me he was undocumented? I knew very little about immigration, and his story hadn't included crossing the border or hiding underneath a train or any other kind of smuggling scenario I'd seen in movies. But I could tell by his tone and the way he'd pushed to finish telling me these details that this information was important.

If he *was* telling me he was undocumented, I knew enough to know that admission was not without risk. Confessing his out-of-date immigration status was a step of trust, and I wanted to treat that disclosure with appropriate seriousness. Still, I wasn't completely sure of the ongoing implications. If this relationship goes anywhere, I thought, I hope he does get that worked out. I assumed Billy's situation was a paperwork issue—like neglecting to update your driver's license within thirty days of moving to a new state. He simply needed to "do it the right way." Maybe he needed to take a half day off work and go to an embassy or someplace and get it all straightened out.

* * *

My lack of knowledge about the details of the immigration system wasn't all that unusual. In 2015, LifeWay Research surveyed evangelicals to ask what influenced their thinking on immigration the most. The number one response was "not sure." Only 12 percent cited the Bible, and 16 percent said they were most influenced by the media. Seventeen percent of respondents did choose "immigrants you have interacted with," which seems encouraging because it suggests that they knew at least one immigrant. But "interacted with" is different than "have a relationship with," and the data leaves unanswered questions about the context and depth of interactions that are influencing how evangelicals think about immigration.[1]

Billy was quickly becoming the biggest influence on my own thinking about the topic. But while overstaying a visa is one common way immigrants might come to live in the States without authorization, Billy's experience was somewhat distinct. It was not motivated by the desperation that characterizes many immigrants' stories. Rather, Billy's story is similar to those of carefree young adults in many parts of the world: young people who seek adventure and new horizons but who pay less attention to paperwork and long-term planning than they should.

Even as his story was unfolding, I recognized how little I knew about how or why immigrants are in the United States illegally. Hot, dusty episodes of forensic dramas had shown me desperate families crossing the U.S.-Mexico border along with gang members and drug cartels. But the factors that influence international migration worldwide are many, and the reasons undocumented immigrants are present in the States can be as unique as the individuals themselves.

Still, generally speaking, migration is characterized by several "push and pull" factors. Push factors are the events and characteristics of the home country that "push" residents to leave. Poverty and lack of jobs are big ones. In Mexico and Central America, trade policies like the 1994 North American Free Trade Agreement (NAFTA) decimated rural farmers, whose corn crops could not complete in the local marketplace against imported U.S. corn, which is subsidized by the federal government.[2] As rural farmers were forced to abandon their livelihoods, they often relocated to nearby urban centers such as Mexico City and Tijuana. Many of them then headed north to the United States to seek employment and find ways to support their families, who often remained back home.

Violence, particularly in Central America, has also been a significant push factor for many families fleeing to the States. In the 1980s and '90s, Nicaragua, El Salvador, and Guatemala were entrenched in bloody civil wars. Guatemala's war took more than two hundred thousand lives and didn't end until 1996, as Billy had reminded me. Similarly, Nicaragua and El Salvador signed peace accords in 1990 and 1992, respectively. Then the rise of local gangs—often in symbiosis with U.S. gangs—unleashed a new season of terror that continues today.[3]

Alexia Salvatierra, a pastor with the Evangelical Lutheran Church in America, told me the story of an evangelical Christian woman who owned a small business in El Salvador and had distant relatives in the States.

> Gang members, who often extort small businesses in the country, came to her and said, "We want $500 from your rich relatives." She couldn't get money from the States, but she scraped together everything she owned and gave them $500. They immediately responded with a demand for $1,000 and the threat that if she called the police, they would 'get her.' She left the house, went a distance away, and called the police. Then the gang members and the police showed up at her house and raped her multiple times.
>
> Her eight-year-old was in the next room, and they told [the woman], "Your daughter is really pretty. She's perfect for selling." So they ran. The mother and her eight-year-old fled El Salvador and entered the U.S.[4]

Salvatierra laments that this mother and daughter are still not safe. Today they are in danger of being deported back to the very country where they were terrorized. Unfortunately, their experience does not guarantee they will be granted permission to stay in the United States for safety, and it is too common a story to elicit any extraordinary response from the immigration officials deciding their fate.

Meanwhile, "pull" factors are the events and characteristics of the destination country that draw immigrants across the border. The American dream has been exported worldwide, and many people are drawn to the life they imagine for themselves in the States. On the surface, it appears to be available to anyone willing to take a risk and work hard. And the reality for many immigrants is that there are more job opportunities in the States than in their home country. Businesses actively recruit Central American workers through local radio and newspaper ads, and offer promises to handle transportation needs and provide visas if immigrants come to work for their company.[5] Connection to family is another strong pull factor. Children, spouses, and siblings are drawn to the States to find and reunite with family members who left years earlier to find work abroad.

* * *

These push and pull factors are only some of the many reasons—collective and personal—that immigrants leave their homes and head to the United States, even if it means entering illegally. But why don't they just come "the right way"? Shouldn't they go through the process and wait in line for legal entry? At a 2017 speech in Texas, U.S. attorney general Jeff Sessions put it this way: "We have a lawful system of immigration. You should do what over one million other immigrants do each year: wait your turn and come lawfully."[6] This comment embodies what many Americans feel. There is a system, and it's okay for the government and the people of the United States to expect people to use it.

While this sentiment may seem straightforward, it sidesteps the outdated nature of our immigration system, which, unfortunately, does not account for the needs of the United States or the needs of immigrants. The reality is this: there are simply very few ways for new arrivals to immigrate legally. "For many would-be immigrants, there is no 'turn' they can wait for, and no line to stand in," write Michelle Mark and Diana Yukari in a 2017 article for *Business Insider*. "The U.S. immigration system is designed to only admit newcomers who fall into very specific categories. If someone falls outside those circumstances, lawful immigration will be challenging, if not impossible."[7]

Three of the legal avenues for immigration are sometimes referred to as "blood, sweat, and tears." These three paths are the primary options for gaining legal permanent residence (commonly known as a green card). "Blood" refers to a U.S. citizen relative applying for an individual to gain status. Priority is given to husbands and wives and to parents applying for their children. However, adult children can also apply for their parents, and siblings can sponsor other siblings. But those petitions are lower on the priority list.

Companies can sponsor immigrants ("sweat") and eventually support their access to legal permanent residence. This avenue is generally reserved for specialized positions that cannot be filled by current U.S. citizens. In fact, each year there are only five thousand visas available for "low-skilled" workers such as farm workers or laborers. To put that number in context, in 1910, approximately five thousand low-skilled workers entered through Ellis Island every day.[8]

Finally, "tears" is the pathway for cases like that of the Salvadoran woman and her daughter who fled to the States for safety. Asylum seekers are running from violence in their home country. Their process is different from that of refugees in that refugees apply for status while outside of the United States. Refugees who are accepted are assigned a new home and offered resettlement support and certain benefits upon arrival. Asylum seekers, on the other hand, apply for protection once they've already arrived in this country. This category is challenging because applicants must prove their life would be in danger if they were to return to their home country, which can be very difficult to demonstrate. If they are approved, they do not receive any benefits or support.

These three options for legal immigration are limited, and many people who do not fit into these narrow categories still come to the United States. They do whatever it takes to protect and provide for their families while taking the risk of a lifetime. Increasingly, these unauthorized travelers are women and children. In 2016, the secretary of Homeland Security noted that "the demographics of illegal migration on our southern border has changed significantly over the last 15 years—far fewer Mexicans and single adults are attempting to cross the border without authorization, but more families and unaccompanied children are fleeing poverty and violence in Central America."[9] In the year between October 2015 and September 2016, almost sixty thousand unaccompanied children were apprehended crossing the southwest U.S. border.[10]

When I consider the desperation of parents who would send their children to cross the border unaccompanied, I think of Moses's mother, who hid her baby from authorities for three months before putting him in a basket in the river, where he floated to safety (Exodus 2:2-5). I think of Mary and Joseph fleeing to Egypt after an angel of the Lord appeared to Joseph in a dream and told him Jesus' life was in danger (Matthew 2:13-15). Parents will do whatever it takes to try to keep their children safe.

Whether you are a child or an adult, crossing the border is literally a life-and-death journey. According to the *New York Times*, the combined number of people killed in Hurricane Katrina and the September 11 terrorist attacks is still fewer than the number of border-crossing deaths between October 2000 and September 2016. During that time, the Border Patrol documented more than six thousand lives lost in the southwestern border states.[11] Migrants from Central America face additional treacherous circumstances while traveling first through Mexico, including risks such as anti–Central American sentiment, corrupt police, gang activity, and the common practice of riding on top of trains to cover large distances quickly.[12]

But sneaking across the border, whether in a major city or in the rugged desert, is not the only way immigrants enter the country illegally. Many pay smugglers, also known as *coyotes*, to serve as guides and bring people safely to the States. Methods may include folding into camouflaged compartments in the trunks of cars, hiding underneath cargo in delivery trucks, traveling underground through the complex system of tunnels that burrow underneath the border, or posing as the children of consenting U.S. couples as they drive home across country lines.

But not everyone is trying to evade law enforcement as they enter the country. Many arrivals, particularly women and children, cross into the country and immediately approach border officials to declare their intent to seek asylum. They are not dodging federal agents. Rather, they are hoping to work with the U.S. government in order to stay legally via the previously mentioned "tears" pathway.

These immigrants have been fleeing violence and terror, and their arrival is a bit like reaching a place of refuge. Here, they hope, they can slow down and announce their arrival. Here, they hope, they can receive a bit of compassion and mercy. Here, they hope, they can rest and heal and begin a new life.

* * *

In another demographic shift, the percentage of undocumented immigrants who arrive in the United States by crossing the border illegally has declined in recent years. Mark Krikorian, the director of the Center for Immigration Studies, notes that estimates in the 1990s approximated that 60 percent of undocumented immigrants had illegally crossed the border. But this vulnerability is no longer the case. "We're much more able than we were before to patrol the border effectively," he writes.[13]

Instead, most current undocumented immigrants in the United States have, like Billy, overstayed their temporary visas. A 2015 study by the Center for Migration Studies found that in each year between 2008 and 2012, the number of people who overstayed their visa exceeded the number of those who had illegally crossed the U.S.-Mexico border.[14] This act is a civil violation of federal immigration law, but is not a criminal offense. The Congressional Research Service explains it like this: "Being illegally present in the U.S. has always been a civil, not criminal, violation of the INA [Immigration and Nationality Act], and subsequent deportation and associated administrative processes are civil proceedings. For instance, a lawfully admitted nonimmigrant alien may become deportable if his visitor's visa expires or if his student status changes."[15]

By 2012, almost 60 percent of all new undocumented immigrants had not crossed the border illegally but rather, as Krikorian states, "are believed to have entered legally on some sort of visa (or visa-waiver status, if they're from a developed country) and then just stayed on after their time expired."[16] A Pew Research Center analysis found that Canadians led the world in unauthorized overstays in the United States at the end of fiscal year 2015, followed by individuals from Mexico, Brazil, Germany, Italy, and the United Kingdom. Still, Canadian overstays far exceeded those from other countries.[17]

Even as trends have shifted toward more undocumented immigrants entering legally, it's important to note that of all the temporary visas issued for business or pleasure, the Department of Homeland Security calculated an overstay rate of only 1.17 percent.[18] In other words, the overwhelming majority of temporary visa holders exit the country within the length of time granted upon their admission.

Billy had cautiously opened up to me about his own immigration story, revealing he was one of the arrivals who had flown into the Los Angeles airport with a valid Guatemalan passport and U.S. travel visa. But when his six-month visit allotment had expired, he'd remained in the country. He was technically no longer allowed to be living or working in the United States.

Since I assumed there was a line he could get into or a way he could work it out, I didn't quite know what to say. Our life experiences, in many ways, seemed so similar that I didn't fully understand how much living in the shadows as an undocumented worker was woven into every part of his daily life. So I didn't say much about his status, simply figuring we could cross that bridge when—or if—we came to it.

4

COYOTE INN

Billy unfolded the map and smoothed it down on the dusty hood of the truck. Moonlight shone on the print of underground utilities. "So tomorrow, this is where you'll need to start," Billy said, tracing the lines of roads, intersections, and pipes. His coworker Oscar nodded. They worked together on an underground drilling crew, installing fiber optics for faster Internet speeds.

Billy surveyed the construction yard, where trucks and equipment were parked overnight. "Everything looks good, man," he clapped Oscar on the back. "Have a good night."

"Will do," Oscar responded. "You too."

"Thanks," Billy said, opening the driver's side door of the company truck. "Not looking forward to this drive, though. Takes me an hour to get home." He tossed his safety vest and the folded maps into the front seat. "I hope I can stay awake! You live close?"

"Oh yeah, man," Oscar nodded. "Me and some of the guys stay here." He gestured toward the warehouse on the property.

"What?" Billy looked around.

"Yeah." Oscar picked up his own vest and hard hat from the ground and turned to walk toward the warehouse. "They got beds and don't charge much."

"Man, that's awesome," Billy laughed. "I'm going to talk to Ramos about that tomorrow!" He offered a final good night before climbing into the truck.

A few days later, Billy strode into the warehouse. Carrying his duffel bag and guitar, he walked past twenty other guys in search of a bunk in his new home. While Billy may have relocated in an effort to reduce his rent and shorten his commute, he soon learned his situation was markedly different from those of his new roommates.

For starters, they had all crossed the border. In bits and pieces, guys would reveal the horrific traumas of their journey: witnessing rapes, seeing gang members stab people, having to leave friends behind in the desert. Most had relied on coyotes, those paid guides who smuggle immigrants across the border. Coyotes are mythical figures in the drama of immigration. Some are trustworthy escorts, lining up transportation and safe houses to shuffle people through the underground pipeline from poverty to promise. Others are notorious for abandoning or exploiting their charges. Once alone in the stark wilderness, a coyote can raise the fee or make demands when immigrants are at their most vulnerable.

Still, many migrants choose to recruit the help of a coyote. The cost to hire such assistance can reach up to $3,000 or $4,000.[1] But many see no other option for a successful crossing, especially since the increase in border enforcement after the Immigration Reform and Control Act of 1986 pushed migrants toward more remote and dangerous routes.[2] Individuals and families standing at the border know that their future, as well as their family's future, hangs in the balance as they make this decision to cross. With no idea of where to find water in the desert and no knowledge of U.S. Border Patrol routes, hiding places, or the location of the nearest city, immigrants who enlist a coyote's guidance may feel that it's the less risky choice. Of course, for poor migrants crossing the border, the fee is completely unreachable.

Enter U.S. businesses. The construction company where Billy worked had paid the smugglers' fees in exchange for the migrants' promise to work for the business until the debt was cleared. Billy's coworkers had taken the deal, and their debt was being deducted from their paychecks right alongside U.S. taxes and Social Security. Many of the laborers had been working for the company for years and were still paying off what they owed. Paying it off felt unrealistic, so workers settled into a rhythm of life. Everyone simply called the warehouse where they now lived and worked "Coyote Inn."

So while Billy was living there voluntarily, the men who were now his roommates were walking a fine line between being smuggled and being trafficked. The legal difference is the use of coercion and exploitation, which takes place in human trafficking, but not when someone has paid a coyote to be smuggled across the border. However, to finance their trip, some migrants end up being hijacked and forced to work in places they never intended or are held captive for ransom.[3]

In fact, according to U.S. Immigration and Customs Enforcement, one question for assessing whether someone is a victim of human trafficking is, "Does the victim owe money to an employer or does the employer hold wages?" Other indicators include "Can the victim freely leave employment or the situation?"; "Does the victim possess identification and travel documents? If not, who has control of these documents?"; and "Did the victim travel to a destination country for a specific job or purpose and is victim engaged in different employment than expected?"[4] It's challenging to collect data on this type of human trafficking, but the International Labour Organization estimates that 1.5 million people are engaged in forced labor in what it calls "developed economies," which include the United States, Canada, and Australia. Forced labor in these economies is estimated to produce $46.9 billion in annual profits.[5]

Labor trafficking occurs throughout the world. It also appears in Scripture, such as when we see Joseph, a seventeen-year-old, sold into slavery by his brothers. He was robbed of his special coat, sold to traveling merchants, and transported against his will to Egypt, where he worked as the overseer of the house of Potiphar (Genesis 37–39). Joseph earned favor in the eyes of his master, but he was still a captive in Potiphar's house, and he later fell victim to false accusations and imprisonment. Such exploitation rings familiar to present-day forced laborers and other undocumented immigrants. While they may experience some successes in work, many discover they are trapped in their employment. Unauthorized immigration status, debts from travel expenses, and threats of violence compound the fragile and vulnerable situation of many immigrants.

* * *

But who is hiring undocumented immigrants? Billy's employment in construction was not his first job since he'd arrived in the States. First he was hired at a factory, packaging women's gloves. Each day, he was expected to arrive at six in the morning to begin his shift. Since he didn't have a vehicle, he got up around three to start his route on L.A.'s public transportation system. At the end of each workday, he would join other employees as they crowded around a posted list to see if they were invited back to work the next day. Billy didn't last long, what with the crushing commute and job instability, and he ended up doing underground construction and contracting for a well-known telecommunications company. He had transitioned to installing satellite dishes when we met, but returned to construction work while we were dating.

In the United States, production (factory work) and construction, along with service jobs, are the top three industries for unauthorized laborers, according to the Pew Research Center. These are followed by transportation and farming.[6] Although fifth in overall industries where immigrants are likely to work, farming stands out at the state level. As the Pew Research Center notes, "Farming is overwhelmingly the occupation where unauthorized immigrants make up the highest share of the workforce. It is the top occupation by this measure in 32 states." In other words, more unauthorized immigrants may work in other industries, but they work a *higher percentage* of total farming jobs.[7]

Take my home state of Kentucky. The data shows that 27 percent of the state's undocumented population works in the service industry, followed by 15 percent in production and 14 percent in farming. However, of farming jobs in the state, 29 percent of them are held by unauthorized immigrants. So most undocumented immigrants in the state are not farm workers, but of farm workers, more than one in four are undocumented immigrants.[8]

It may be unsurprising to learn that some specific occupations—such as drywall installers, roofers, construction painters, and agricultural workers—have a high percentage of undocumented workers. Still, despite the concentration of unauthorized employees in these jobs, U.S.-born workers still account for the majority of all these positions.[9] It's also important to note that unauthorized immigrant workers are found in a variety of other occupations, including software developers, chefs, and office and administrative support staff.[10]

The logistics behind hiring undocumented immigrants are tricky to pin down and likely vary by industry and employer. Some workers provide incorrect Social Security numbers, and employers either don't know or choose not to look closely. Most of these employees are receiving legitimate paychecks and are contributing the same payroll taxes as U.S. citizens, including Social Security and Medicaid. Some employers pay in cash and avoid an official hiring process altogether. This under-the-table payment is what many U.S. citizens assume is the typical procedure. However, most of the undocumented immigrants I've met were not being paid in cash but were actually on payroll with their employers.

These workarounds, utilized by both employees and employers, are used in both positive and negative ways. Sometimes compassionate employers look the other way because they know they are supporting a person (and that person's family) who deeply needs the opportunity to work. Of course, this underground employment also opens the door for extreme injustice, exploitation, and abuse. For example, the *New York Times* interviewed 150 workers and owners in the nail salon industry and discovered that "a vast majority of workers are paid below minimum wage; sometimes they are not even paid. Workers endure all manner of humiliation, including having their tips docked as punishment for minor transgressions, constant video monitoring by owners, even physical abuse."[11]

In 2011, the *Los Angeles Times* told the story of Josue Melquisedec Diaz, a New Orleans day laborer who was picked up and taken just across the Louisiana state line into Texas to help with Hurricane Gustav cleanup. The area was contaminated with standing water and dead animals. When Diaz and other undocumented workers requested safety equipment, such as gloves and masks, which had been provided to the nonimmigrant workers, their pay was slashed in half. Diaz and the others stopped work, and before long, police and immigration officials showed up to detain the workers.[12]

The book of Genesis tells us that Joseph also ended up in prison. After Joseph refused the sexual demands of Potiphar's wife, she took advantage of her position and falsely accused him. He was wrongly imprisoned and spent years behind bars. Forgotten by a former cellmate, who promised him a favor, he sat in his cell, still waiting for God's next steps for his life.

* * *

It didn't take long before Billy was suffocating in the conditions of Coyote Inn. Empty beer bottles lined up on the floor, and puffs of marijuana smoke wafted through the air. Guys clustered in groups, playing cards and laughing too loud. One by one, men slipped away, squinting at international calling cards as they leaned into nearby pay phones.

Billy had been overwhelmed by the construction work when he started. His family in Guatemala was middle class, and he'd had zero experience in manual labor. Billy had received his post–high school certification in electronics, but his dream had been to see the ministry of his band grow and to use his love of music to serve.

But the jobs available to him as an undocumented worker in the United States were different from those for which his upbringing and training had prepared him. So, instead, he'd found himself on the side of road in Los Angeles, asking fellow laborers to show him how to use a jackhammer. His muscles had ached from the physical labor, and he had to build his strength and endurance to keep up with the rest of the crew.

At Coyote Inn, Billy wandered over to a small closet along the wall. Inside he found empty boxes, discarded bubble wrap, and leftover equipment. He immediately began pulling out the trash and breaking down boxes.

"¿Qué haces?" one guy hollered. What are you doing? But Billy put in his headphones and continued to unpack and clean. He swept out the closet before finally sliding his mattress off his bunk and dragging it over to the door.

"Seriously, man. Whatchu doing?" A guy ambled over from a nearby TV.

"I'm moving in here," Billy told him. "I need my own space." He stood the mattress up in the doorframe and pushed it into place. His new living quarters were so tight that he couldn't walk on either side of the mattress, so he'd essentially fall onto it from the doorway each night. But he was grateful to have some barrier from the desperation on the other side of the door.

Billy slept in that closet for one year. In quiet moments, he seriously questioned what he was doing and where God was hiding. This was not the future he had imagined for himself. But he also felt trapped. Going back to Guatemala, where there was no work waiting for him, seemed like failing. Surely he could push through for a little longer, save a little money, and go back home to start his own business. Or maybe he should look for something else in the States. But moving out of his situation felt unlikely, given that he had no one and nowhere to go to. Plus, he had little time to look for a new job.

So Billy continued putting one foot in front of the other, doing whatever it took to get experience and learning as quickly as possible. He constantly asked coworkers to teach him new skills: how to use the drilling machine, how to navigate underground utilities. He used his background in electronics to figure out how to read the underground prints detailing the gas, water, and power line routes.

And this manic work ethic was soon rewarded. He became the general manager of the construction company where he'd started out as a laborer. Because he wanted to do anything besides be in that warehouse, Billy crossed the parking lot and was in the office by five in the morning, doing paperwork and making sure crews had everything they needed for the day. During the day, he was out in the field, overseeing the sites and helping to drill. At night, he returned to the office to complete payroll, communicate with vendors to order supplies, and prepare for the morning. He often stayed until midnight, working nearly nineteen hours a day, six or seven days a week. {

Billy was working in construction while we were dating.

When Billy shared with me these experiences of his first jobs in the United States, I was dumbfounded. Commuting six hours a day to a factory? Not knowing if you'd have work the next day? Using machinery without any safety training? Living in a closet? It made my summer rehanging dresses in the juniors' department seem like a vacation. His was a world of work that was completely unfamiliar to me.

But it is not uncommon for immigrant workers to log long hours in dangerous conditions. In fact, our economy depends on it. After the September 11 tragedy rocked the United States, citizens were told that the most effective way they could support the country was to shop. The goal was to lift the United States out of a fearful slump that had consumers staying home and tightening their purse strings. Our economy relies on constant consumption. To keep this cycle afloat, we require a steady stream of new products, services, and consumables at affordable prices. We need cheap, disposable clothes. We need low grocery prices and ready-to-eat food options. We need shiny new technology that fuels constant replacements and upgrades. These pillars of the U.S. economy are sustained by an international labor force at home and abroad that harvests natural resources, produces cheap goods, and provides cheap labor to keep those plates spinning.

But amid this frantic cycle of production and consumption, I was struck by the inhumanity that was woven through the stories of undocumented immigrants working in this economy. Of course broader issues were at play, with immigration laws and the workers and employers in violation of them. But I could not escape a deep, core belief that, at the end of the day, the people picking apples, grooming horses, cleaning houses, and drilling to install fiber optics for Internet service were humans made in the image of God. How do we as people of faith—who are also

Lexington Public Library

www.lexpublib.org
(859) 231-5500

**********0306

Number of items:

1

Barcode:0000226235729
Title:Love undocumented : risking trust in a
fearful world /
Due:4/23/2019

3/26/2019   6:16 PM

To renew items:
Call (859) 231-5500
or visit www.lexpublib.org

business owners, shoppers, and neighbors—affirm the humanity of those in the shadows of our workforce?

* * *

"I was in a bad place at that time in my life," Billy told me as we sat on a metal bench in the quaint downtown of a small Los Angeles suburb. Saturday shoppers sauntered in and out of gift shops with window displays of wind chimes and signs that said things like "Sorry for the mess; we live here."

"Even working all the time, I was so lonely," Billy said. He talked about how much he'd missed his family and friends at home. He described that season as a time that challenged his faith, a time when he felt so disconnected from and abandoned by a God he believed had called him to serve. I listened to how unsettling Billy's experience had been for him, and I thought about other immigrants who perhaps didn't feel that they had any choice but to come to the States or who had endured trauma in the process. Starting over in a new land with unfamiliar customs and possibly an unknown language can be jolting. The transition had even shaken Billy's connection with God.

"How did you leave that job?" I asked, wondering how so much had changed between the time he was describing and when we'd started dating. He was now installing satellite dishes during what seemed to be regular business hours, and he was even able to head out early enough to meet me for dinner a couple of nights a week.

"Well, it was getting more and more shady. My boss started waking me up in the middle of the night to come unload trucks full of what I assumed were stolen electronics. Also, other guys had started to talk bad about me to the boss, and I knew I needed to get out of there. So I found another job. But when my boss, Ramos, heard I might be leaving, he called me to his office."

Billy described this conversation, and how his boss began to scream and berate him. At one point, Ramos grew so enraged that he picked up a bicycle that was leaning against the wall and threw it. "He thought it was my bicycle," Billy said, smiling. "He was kicking it and going crazy. What he didn't know was that I had sold it to another supervisor. When he was finished kicking it, I told him, 'That's not my bicycle anymore. It's Juanito's.'" But this new information only made Ramos more upset. "Bottom line," Billy concluded, "Ramos didn't think I would find another job and actually leave."

But Billy did leave. His brother had relocated to the States, so Billy moved in with him. Together they had begun installing cable TV, and this work was much less demanding. Around the same time, Billy began to tentatively reach out to God.

"One day I showed up at a big church near where I was living. They had a young adults group after the service, and I stayed. I knew I would never really walk away from God, but I was so confused and angry. And lonely. So I just showed up and started talking to people."

The church welcomed Billy back into a connection with God, as well as into a family of believers. His experiences as a laborer may have capitalized on his capacity to produce, his limited complaining, and his willingness to do whatever was needed. But the young adults at his new church saw him first as a friend and fellow follower of Christ, not as a one-dimensional undocumented immigrant.

They invited him to participate in a "Surfers for Christ" group that met at the beach on the weekends to ride the waves and build relationships with other surfers. Billy went. "I'm forever grateful to those folks," he told me. "When life felt crazy, they helped me stay connected to the person I really was and the God that I loved." God's grace and presence was manifest to him through a body of believers. They met Billy exactly where he was and reminded him of the plans God had for his life.

In Genesis, Joseph must have also felt forgotten by God as he waited in prison. He had interpreted a dream for the pharaoh's cupbearer, who was also in prison, and Joseph had asked him to help secure his release, but two years went by. Finally, when the pharaoh had a dream no one could interpret, the cupbearer remembered the young Hebrew, locked away, who had a gift for interpreting dreams. Pharaoh sent for Joseph, and after hearing his interpretation regarding the forthcoming years of plenty followed by famine, was pleased with Joseph's plan for addressing the issue. Pharaoh told him, "Since God has shown you all this, there is none so discerning and wise as you are. You shall be over my house, and all my people shall order themselves as you command. Only as regards the throne will I be greater than you" (Genesis 41:39-40).

God had not forgotten Billy. God had not forgotten Joseph. God has not forgotten the millions of immigrants living in the shadows. I was deeply moved as I listened to Billy's stories. I had never really considered the ins and outs of how immigrants survived behind the curtain of their out-of-status existence in the country. Their invisibility had allowed me not to notice the buffer of distance. And this disconnect made it difficult for me to connect to God's image in the Other.

But in so many ways, Billy and I were still just scratching the surface. I had much more to learn about life without authorized status. As our individual stories continued to intertwine, I was about to become more involved in the plotline of immigration than I ever expected.

5

RED FLAGS

*I*nky darkness danced between the houses on the quiet cul-de-sac where Billy now shared a house with his brother and sister-and-law and another friend. Except for the radio, the car was off, and I leaned back in my seat while Billy talked. "I met someone today when I was working," he told me. "He started asking about my immigration status, and then he gave me this." Billy pulled a business card from his wallet and pushed it toward me.

I studied the detailed seal that I did not recognize, the raised font naming an immigration attorney followed by a series of important-looking initials. I ran my finger over the name. "I just don't know," Billy said, verbalizing the question I was thinking but hadn't yet asked. "I don't know if I can trust this guy. I mean, he's a stranger. What if it's a scam? What if I call this lawyer and he turns me in?"

I knew Billy's concerns were valid. We'd both heard the stories: scam artists preying on vulnerable immigrants who attempted to reconcile their status. Actor Diane Guerrero, who had roles on *Jane the Virgin* and *Orange Is the New Black*, details in her memoir how her parents worked to adjust their

immigration status legally. Her father hired a lawyer on the rec-
ommendation of a neighbor. The lawyer told him his case was
challenging, given that he'd emigrated from Colombia and had
no U.S. citizen relatives besides his middle-school-aged daughter. Still, the lawyer promised to help and started Guerrero's dad
on a monthly payment plan. Her father took on a third job,
and they worked to make the regular payments on time. Every
month, her father checked the status of his case and was told
they were getting closer to a resolution. Then, after a couple of
unreturned phone calls, Guerrero and her father showed up at
the lawyer's office.

"The room was dark," she writes. "The lawyer's desk was
gone. In a corner sat a stack of cardboard boxes and some rolls
of packing tape. Old newspapers lay scattered across the floor.
Except for the nail upon which the Lady Justice picture had
hung, the walls were totally bare. I turned to Papi, whose brown
eyes widened. He put his hand on his head. '*No lo puedo creer*,'
he murmured almost inaudibly. 'I can't believe it.'"[1]

Stories like Guerrero's are all too common, and this fear of
betrayal is one reason it is difficult to convince undocumented
immigrants to take advantage of legal pathways that may be
available to them. In 1986, when President Ronald Reagan
signed the Immigration Reform and Control Act (IRCA) into
law, it included language that allowed undocumented immigrants access to legalization.[2] Almost three million immigrants adjusted their status through this legislation. Yet there
were still immigrants too afraid to come forward and address
their status. They were worried—for good reason—about being
bamboozled.

More recently, on June 15, 2012, the secretary of Homeland
Security announced the Deferred Action for Childhood
Arrivals (DACA) program. Young adults who met specific

criteria were allowed to request consideration of deferred action from deportation. According to archived information on the U.S. Citizenship and Immigration Services website, "Deferred action is a use of prosecutorial discretion to defer removal action against an individual for a certain period of time. Deferred action does not provide lawful status."[3] Essentially, undocumented immigrants who had been brought to the United States before age sixteen, were in school or had graduated (or were honorably discharged veterans of the U.S. Armed Forces), and had not been convicted of a felony could apply. These young people are often known as "Dreamers," in reference to the DREAM Act, a legislative proposal that sought to provide similar protections for young immigrants but was not passed by Congress.

DACA was not amnesty, as many critics claimed. Legal status adjustment wasn't even an option. Instead, applicants were simply being considered for work authorization and protection from deportation for two years. Still, in a 2016 campaign speech in Phoenix, presidential candidate Donald Trump promised to "immediately terminate" DACA, which he referred to as an illegal executive amnesty.[4] When he won the election, many DACA recipients became terrified not only of the potential end of the program, which had offered them temporary relief, but also because they had registered with the government in good faith, submitting personal information and data that could now be used against them. In September 2017, the Trump administration rescinded DACA and gave Congress six months to pursue a legislative solution. Without action, almost eight hundred thousand people will again be at risk for deportation. As of this writing, the fate of the Dreamers was unclear.[5]

* * *

Billy pulled the business card from my hands, an edge of frustration in his action. "I just want to be able to fix this," he muttered, stuffing it into his wallet. I knew Billy's status adjustment was more complex than I had originally assumed. It was not a problem that could be solved by taking a number and waiting in line at a government office. Still, I was uncertain what the whole process really involved.

"I know," I said, weakly trying to offer support. "Maybe it's worth a call? Maybe this person could help you know what your next step is?"

He looked out the window. Suddenly he turned toward me and let out a torrent of words. "I already know what he'll say. I have already talked to people. Everyone is telling me the same thing. There is nothing I can do. There's nothing to be done! Well, there's only one thing I can do, but there's nothing *really* I can do. I want to be able to take care of this on my own. I don't want you involved. I don't want to put you in that position. I just want to be able to do this on my own, and it's so frustrating."

I tilted my head, and my mouth pulled to the side. I was confused. It must have shown, because Billy took a deep breath before calmly relating the full story. "The only way I can fix my papers is if I marry a U.S. citizen. You are a citizen. But I hate that. And I don't want you to think that's why I'm dating you. In fact, if you think that"—his voice got louder and his words got faster—"we should break up now. I'm serious. I don't want you to ever think that, and it makes me so upset. I wish there was something I could do to fix this on my own. But there isn't. So I think we should just break up."

I leaned back in my seat and gazed out the front windshield. I almost wanted to laugh. What had just happened? I'd had no idea his only pathway to adjust his status was to marry a citizen, to marry me. Of course I didn't think that's why he was dating me! And we'd only been dating a couple of months. While I knew our relationship was serious, I wasn't ready to declare marriage. I also wasn't ready to break up.

* * *

"I don't understand what you don't understand. *They broke the law.*" This general sentiment underscores a great deal of Internet comments, as well as remarks in real-life conversations on immigration. It is a justifiable response from the outside looking in. Many Christians may feel legitimately sorry for foreigners suffering under unspeakable conditions in their countries of origin. They may also experience the pull of pity with regard to the oppressive and exploitative conditions in which undocumented immigrants work in the States. But many stop short of grappling with God's directive to seek justice for the poor and welcome the stranger because of their loyalty to laws of the state and a reliance on biblical passages that instruct us to respect governing authorities.

The apostle Paul expresses this so clearly in Romans 13:1-5, quoted here in Eugene Peterson's paraphrase, *The Message*:

> Be a good citizen. All governments are under God. Insofar as there is peace and order, it's God's order. So live responsibly as a citizen. If you're irresponsible to the state, then you're irresponsible with God, and God will hold you responsible. Duly constituted authorities are only a threat if you're trying to get by with something. Decent citizens should have nothing to fear.
>
> Do you want to be on good terms with the government? Be a responsible citizen and you'll get on just fine, the government working to your advantage. But if you're breaking the rules right and left, watch out. The police aren't there just to be admired in their uniforms. God also has an interest in keeping order, and

he uses them to do it. That's why you must live responsibly—not just to avoid punishment but also because it's the right way to live.

As a lifelong rule-follower, I resonate with these verses. Once, in the third grade, I looked at a friend's paper during a test and saw an answer to one question. When I received my graded exam, I'd aced it, but I was overcome with guilt about my glance at that one answer. I immediately confessed my sin to my teacher, who responded by scribbling out my score and ripping the sticker from the top of the paper, leaving a small tear. My eight-year-old heart was broken, but I also felt relieved. I hated feeling that I had broken the rules, and this pattern has continued into my adulthood.

As Christ-followers, we seek to honor the laws of the land in which we live while recognizing that our primarily allegiance is to God. When asylum seekers—like the mother and child we met in chapter 3—escape immediate danger and flee to the United States, have they violated God's law? How do we reconcile Scriptures that suggest God sets authorities such as police in place to maintain God's order with stories of assault and brutality from those same officers? In many cases, including those of unaccompanied children who arrive at the border fleeing violence, the United States has denied asylum status. As a country, the United States has the prerogative to reject refugees and asylum seekers. But as Christians, we must hold the laws of the state under the light of God's laws. When we turn away the victimized, the lonely, and the poor, has the United States respected God's laws? Can we as Christians support those actions? How do we balance respect for our governing authorities with the perspective of vulnerable parents and children being sent back into life-threatening danger?

These questions are not easy to wrestle through, and situations are often more complex than we imagine. While it may feel easier to simply say that people should follow the law, we must recognize that laws are not infallible and that they have fluctuated and changed greatly over the years. For example, it's interesting to note that there were essentially no limits on legal immigration from Latin America before 1965.[6] In fact, not only were there relatively few restrictions on legal immigration, but the United States also hosted a robust and active temporary worker program.

While World War II was raging abroad and many American men were fighting in Europe, the railways and farms at home were languishing without workers. So in 1942, the United States recruited Mexican workers to migrate north as temporary, seasonal workers, thus initiating the first iteration of what has come to be known as the Bracero Program (the Spanish term *bracero* means "manual laborer"). This agreement between the governments of Mexico and the United States had clear expectations for how Mexican workers would be paid and treated and what their rights included. The U.S. government was open to these demands in the midst of such a significant labor shortage. The second Bracero Program began in 1948, the year after the first one ended, and extended until 1964. More than 4.5 million Mexican workers traveled back and forth to the States, primarily working in agriculture.[7]

The year after the Bracero Program ended, the Immigration and Nationality Act was passed, limiting legal immigration from Mexico. The Migration Policy Institute notes the effect of this nearly simultaneous change in relationship. "When the guestworker program ended, many former Bracero workers continued crossing the border to fill the same jobs, but now illegally. The combination of the end of the Bracero program and limits on legal immigration from the Western Hemisphere combined to fuel the rise of illegal immigration."[8] For twenty-two years, workers had been legally crossing the border, working needed jobs, and returning home. After legislative changes, those same Mexican workers returned to their seasonal jobs, but they were now in violation of the law. Dramatic changes in the law had a significant impact on the workers who had relied on those jobs to support their families.

Immigration law is designed from the top down. The interests of those with the least to lose are given top priority. Politicians and local leaders approach the subject from the perspective of "What do we need from immigrants?" or "What will best serve the country/state/city?" This approach is not new or shocking. Some would argue that it is the role of government to legislate this way. It is, after all, typical of how most laws are created.

* * *

When I led a Sociology 101 discussion group for undergraduates at the University of Kentucky, I had my students play the StarPower game.[9] For those who never had a sociology teacher who loved interactive classroom activities, let me explain. The game begins with each student receiving an envelope filled with squares of colored paper. Each color has a different assigned value, and every student gets a unique combination of colored squares.

Some ground rules are established to allow the students to make trades with others in an attempt to increase their overall net worth. Students scuttle around the room, happily making deals and standing their ground. At the end of round one, everyone is grouped according to the value of their envelopes after trading. Then round two begins. When students form groups at the end of this round, few people have changed groups. Now comes the twist! The group with the highest wealth is applauded for their hard work and surprised with the opportunity to change the trading rules. Almost without exception, this group adjusts the rules drastically in their favor. They easily decimate the remainder of the class in just a few more rounds.

I always led this game in a short, fifty-minute class, but I had to be intentional about leaving time to debrief. Students were often visibly upset. It was not uncommon for those who'd felt most taken advantage of to be angry or despondent and to declare, "This game is stupid." Those in the top group were giddy, or perhaps embarrassed by their game behavior. One of the exemplified truths of this interactive experiment is that it is our human nature to make rules (laws) in our own self-interest. Power abuse and oppression are not surprising.

When we see immigration law functioning for the benefit of those in power rather than for those who most need relief, opportunity, and care, it is hardly an anomaly. And while we may think this is the appropriate role of the government—to construct immigration laws that bring the greatest benefit to our own country—we must acknowledge that the kingdom of God calls us to different concerns, values, allegiances, and actions.

From the moment he arrived and was laid in a manger, Jesus has been challenging his followers to be present and active on behalf of the most vulnerable. This is a countercultural way to live when we are most accustomed to everyone seeking only their own best interests. Instead, we are told in Scripture to pay attention to those on the margins of power who are the most vulnerable. We are instructed to leave extra grain at the edges of our fields rather than take all our profits for ourselves. And as the people of God, we are reminded of our own experiences as foreigners. We hear a call for mercy and welcome in the midst of a society that exploits and abuses those who are not "their own."

* * *

Still, it is an inescapable fact that undocumented immigrants are in violation of federal laws. Regardless of whether they crossed the border unlawfully, or they failed to exit within the boundaries of a legal visa, or a parent made the choice for them: those who are undocumented are breaking a law. This status of rule-breaking is a chasm too wide across for some Christians to reach.

Yet our call to love extends beyond our feelings of affection or our satisfied inquiries into whether another person is deserving of our care. We are challenged to love our enemies and pray for those who persecute us (Matthew 5:44), and we are told to love others because God loved us (1 John 4:19). Theologian William Willimon, in his book *Fear of the Other*, writes, "We simply try to see the Other as loved and cherished by God in the Other's mix of righteousness and sin, good and evil, *as are we*, embraced by the outstretched hands of Christ on the cross."[10] We open our arms to immigrants, documented or not, not on the basis of their purity or deservingness but because of Christ's love for us in our undeservingness.

Jesus demonstrates this unconditional love to those he meets who had broken laws, including Zacchaeus, the Samaritan woman, and the man crucified next to him at Golgotha. We also witness his mercy in John 8, when the scribes and the Pharisees introduce him to a woman caught in adultery. They question Jesus, saying, "Now in the Law, Moses commanded us to stone such women. So what do you say?" (John 8:5). Jesus bends down to draw in the dirt. "And as they continued to ask him, he stood up and said to them, 'Let him who is without sin among you be the first to throw a stone at her'" (verse 7). Then he returns to writing in the ground until everyone has walked away. Of course, that's not the end of the story. Jesus sends the woman off with the famous parting words, "Neither do I condemn you; go, and from now on sin no more" (verse 11).

A friend of mine who pastors in a heavily immigrant area once shared his perspective on counseling undocumented immigrants. He explains that if a family member's life is at risk, whether because of violence or poverty or other circumstance, he cannot encourage them to return home. In these situations, he tries to support them in adjusting their status, if at all possible, through the narrow channels available. If a person is in violation of the law and is in the States out of preference or desire, he says, he encourages them to return home. Having options in their home country makes a difference in how he counsels them.

This nuanced perspective made a lot of sense to me. But it did cause me to question Billy's circumstances, which certainly fell into the latter category. I knew Billy felt conflicted about his undocumented status. On the one hand, he still had a ten-year visa, and the fact that he had simply forgotten to renew his time allotment made him feel that his unauthorized status was the unfortunate result of simple oversight. On the other hand, he also knew he was an undocumented immigrant, and he didn't like living in that tension. If we hadn't started dating and taking tentative steps toward marriage, it's extremely likely he would have left the United States on his own. As time had gone by, Billy saw no real future for himself in the United States, and he did have options in his home country.

* * *

In 2011, Alabama was frustrated with the federal government's delay on addressing immigration reform. So the state decided to take matters into its own hands and passed HB 56, the Beason-Hammon Alabama Taxpayer and Citizen Protection Act. Considered the harshest state immigration law in the country, the legislation contained language that made it a crime to transport, harbor, or conceal an unauthorized alien. Expressly explained as an attempt to curb human trafficking, the wording was broad and vague enough in nature to raise a lot of questions, particularly for Christians. Was it now a crime to drive an undocumented immigrant to the grocery store or to the doctor or to church? If you had someone over to your house for a meal without checking their immigration status, was that considered harboring or concealing?

Legal challenges to much of the legislation immediately ensued, preventing many sections from going into effect. However, the Trump administration has breathed new life into some of the measures, even tapping former Alabama senator Jeff Sessions, who supported HB 56, for attorney general of the United States.

Following the law is important. It is a responsibility of the people of God. However, as we recall how many of Jesus' disciples were martyred and killed by the state—Bartholomew, James, Peter, and more—we must recognize that the law of God and the laws of the state do not always align. As immigration laws continue to shift and change—whether at the state level or the federal level—Christians are faced with a choice. What will we do if Christlike behavior becomes criminalized? Will we avoid hospitality in an effort to sidestep the potential for breaking laws? Or will we do what is right even if it challenges the law?

* * *

"I think we should just break up." Billy's final words hung in the air.

I considered everything he'd told me about his immigration status since we'd started dating. How he'd introduced his undocumented status early in our relationship. How I'd now learned that I was his pathway to legalization. How this situation frustrated him beyond imagination, and how he'd rather break up than have his motives come under suspicion.

What if he *was* cozying up to me with the hope of eventually adjusting his immigration status? I mulled it over, but the whole idea felt ridiculous. Other versions of the same question wafted through my thoughts. What if I was being used or taken advantage of? What if my compassion and optimistic belief in people was being twisted for his personal gain? It's one thing to take steps in the direction of love for someone else. But another's motives are outside our control and may not always be pure. That's always a possibility in reaching out toward another person.

As I considered Billy's revelation, I kept coming back to the idea that any relationship involves risk. Does this person like me as much as I like them? Are they using me for some other reason? Will they hurt me? Immigration may have been a third wheel in our courtship, but so much of dating is getting to know who the other person is. That this guy in his twenties hadn't exactly been on top of the details and paperwork of his life wasn't all that mind-blowing. And nothing I'd learned about Billy and his character suggested that he would try to deceive me and manipulate me for his own benefit. In fact, my getting to know him had showed me that Billy was a man of integrity and faith.

"Okay." I spoke slowly and turned to face Billy. He stared at his lap. I reached across the console to hug him. "I don't think that's why you're dating me," I assured him. "I didn't know anything about this, and I don't think we need to break up."

I felt his shoulders relax, and he hugged me back. He sat back to look at me. "Let's just take it easy and play it by ear," I said. "Maybe your friends are wrong."

He nodded, and I squeezed his hand. "We'll figure it out," I promised.

6

COUGH SYRUP AND SANDWICHES

I don't know . . ." I wavered, trying to be polite while also semi crab-walking backward and away from the man on his knees pushing the spoon toward my mouth.

"Sarita," Billy's dad implored, with equal parts playful teasing and gruff annoyance. "Pro . . . bá . . . lo." He stressed the middle syllable. My Spanish was weak, but I knew he was telling me, "Try it."

I looked at his face, tanned and weathered. His dark eyes peered at me through glasses, and his gray mustache covered his lips. I weighed my options. Cuty—pronounced *Cootee*, not "cutie" like I'd first thought—would potentially be my father-in-law one day, and I didn't want to be known as that spoiled American girl who rejected his kind offer of homemade medical remedies.

On the other hand, we'd met only a couple of weeks before when he and his wife, Lucky, had picked me up at the airport in Guatemala City. The trip to Guatemala in order to learn Spanish, which I'd discussed with Billy when we'd first met, had come to fruition. When my roommate and I landed, we were greeted at the airport by Lucky—pronounced *Lookey*— smiling, waving, and holding a sign that read "Sarita We Love." This diminutive of my name was a common, endearing practice and translated loosely to "little Sarah." We'd rolled our luggage toward her. "Sarita!" Lucky had yelled with delight, wrapping me in a tight hug and kissing my cheek twice before leading us away from the airport toward the car.

Guatemala was a country that embraced you. In my fatigued, didn't-really-sleep-all-night-long-on-the-plane state, I had been jolted awake by overwhelming stimuli. Vendors held beaded parrot keychains in front of me as we tried to walk away from the crowds. Exhaust plumed from passing cars, every one of which seemed to go ahead and honk a couple of times for good measure. My eyes watered, and I wiped away the baby tears, as well as the tiny smear of lipstick still kissing me on the cheek. I was reminded of that first day in MacArthur Park: crowded, loud, and full of dissonant smells.

I stood a little taller and yanked my giant suitcase up over the curb and onto the sidewalk. I'd been in Los Angeles for almost a year, and the city had become a bit like an older sister, one who'd held my hand and led me into a bigger world than I'd ever known. She'd introduced me to diverse characters from all over the globe. And without me realizing it, she'd made me more comfortable, less fearful, and more open to adventure. True, I had Billy's mom as a guide, shooing away vendors with a confident hand and rapid Spanish. But at least I wasn't searching for a hidden staircase.

Once all four of us squeezed into the cab of Cuty's truck, Lucky turned to me. "Sarita, I am so glad you here," she said in deliberate English. "When Billy tell me"—she pronounced Billy like Bee-lee—"that you are coming here for to learn Spanish, I tell him you come first to my house to take a rest, eat, and we take you later to school."

They welcomed us into their home, filled us with deliciously sugared coffee, and offered their own bed to sleep in after the tiring flight. Then they made lunch before driving us to the bus station and helping us navigate all the details for our trip to language school in a city a few hours away. Apparently I was the only one who thought it the least bit awkward to fly to a new country and hang out with a boyfriend's parents without him there. So at Billy's suggestion, and my hosts' gracious insistence, I returned to Lucky and Cuty's house a couple of weeks later. Unfortunately, I arrived with a nasty cough, but it was nothing Cuty couldn't handle with a squirt of lime, a little honey, and some suck-it-up determination.

I eyed his gooey spoonful nervously, preferring my Robitussin standby to whatever he'd whipped up on the fly. At the same time, I knew we were only a couple of moments from him swooping it through the air and making full-on airplane noises. Lucky stood over his shoulder, laughing and assuring me, "Sarita, don't worry. Is fine." My best option appeared to be simply closing my eyes and opening my mouth. Cuty seized the opportunity and fed me like a baby. I slurped and swallowed.

"¡Guácala!" I exclaimed. One of my most confident Spanish words, it was essentially Guatemalan slang for "Ew! Yuck!"

Lucky clapped her hands and exclaimed, "Ay! That's Billy!"

I looked up at her. Her hands were clasped together underneath her chin. She reached out and grabbed my face. "Guácala . . . that's Billy!"

"Yeah, Billy taught me that," I confirmed, though no one had seemed in doubt. Lucky kissed me on the cheek. Her eyes watered as she murmured my boyfriend's name. In my mouth, she had heard her son.

* * *

I knew Lucky and Cuty had not seen Billy for almost three years. For many families in which one or more members emigrate, long-term family separation is a reality. In a study of 385 early adolescent immigrants, researchers found that 85 percent of participants had experienced separation from one or both parents for an extended period of time.[1] And while this type of disconnection is always difficult, the separation frequently lasts much longer than families originally anticipate. A mom might plan to return to her home country or send for a child once she's saved up enough money, but high expenses overtax her low wages, and saving happens much more slowly than she expected.

For some parents, when they are eventually reunited with their children, there is tension and unforeseen struggles. In the book *Enrique's Journey*, journalist Sonia Nazario traces the life story of Enrique, a Honduran teen whose mother left for the States when he was only five.[2] She had only planned to be gone one year. When Enrique experiences multiple rejections from family members entrusted with his care, he begins to fantasize about joining her. After a brutal journey, he locates his mother, her new boyfriend, and his half sister, but Enrique struggles to fit into their family. Anger and resentment spill from Enrique, which are an affront to his mother, who believes she should be respected for the sacrifices she made for him. Their fights expose a rift in need of great healing. *Enrique's Journey* speaks to the real challenges immigrant families face when separated and also when reunited.

In Lucky's case, all three of her adult children and an additional four grandchildren were living in the States. Regardless of a child's age, it is painful to be apart. I thought about how

Billy's parents, Lucky and Cuty (shown here with two of their grand-children), showed me hospitality during my stay in Guatemala.

difficult my move to L.A. had been for me and for my family, who lived so far away in Kentucky. Given Billy's undocumented status, he was unable to return and visit his parents. Instead, it was me, the American girlfriend, who had mostly recently sung "Happy Birthday" over tres leches cake for her granddaughter, held her newborn grandson, whom she'd not yet met, and kissed her son, whom she hadn't seen in years.

Lucky held my face in her hands. She had offered me her food, her coffee, her welcome, and her affection. Cuty had told me he was looking out for me, and he'd spoon-fed me home-made cough syrup. Their hospitality had enveloped me and made me feel welcome in this new country.

At the same time, the unfolding scene was so much bigger than just the three of us in that room. By caring for me, Lucky was also revealing how much she loved and missed her son.

* * *

Isn't that how Scripture paints the bigness of hospitality? We are not just welcoming the stranger; through our care we are actually demonstrating our love for God. Too often we associate hospitality with inviting someone over for dinner or hosting our friends for Pinterest-inspired theme parties. There's nothing wrong with those things, of course. But the word *hospitality* in the Bible comes from the Greek word *philoxenia*, which is defined by *Strong's Concordance* as "love to strangers."[3]

What does it mean to show love to strangers? What does hospitality look like? Perhaps it means offering them your bed after a long flight. Perhaps it means whipping up home remedies when you learn they are in pain. Perhaps it looks like holding someone's face in your hands and thinking, "You help me remember someone I care about."

Jesus is often described as a migrant or stranger. Right from the start, he was born in a city far from his parents' home (Luke 2). Then, while he was still very young, his family fled to Egypt to escape persecution from King Herod and save Jesus' life (Matthew 2). And by the time he began his ministry, Jesus traveled from place to place, often relying on the warm and open welcome of the people he encountered. What if when we engage strangers we saw Jesus in their eyes, felt him in their touch, and heard God in their mouths? How quick would we be to show love and offer hospitality to the stranger?

The good Samaritan (Luke 10) is an all-time favorite biblical illustration of caring for the stranger. In this story, a Jewish man is beaten and bloodied by the road. Two other Jewish men walk by. In fact, they are respected Jewish leaders, but they bypass their brother and even cross to the other side, possibly preoccupied with ritual cleanliness and their personal responsibilities.

And then we see the Samaritan—a member of a people group despised by the Jews—who serves as the example of how to care for our neighbor. He offers personal attention, medical provision, transportation, shelter, and financial support. The injured Jew is a stranger to him, but he responds with bighearted hospitality. Jesus uses this story to answer the question, "Who is my neighbor?" At the end of the telling, he poses the same question to the man who originally asked it: "Who was the neighbor to the injured man?" The man has only one response, of course: the one who showed mercy.

I can't help but think Jesus' listener—an expert in religious law—felt a little sheepish when he had to declare the despised foreigner the hero of the story. In his book *Christians at the Border*, M. Daniel Carroll R. explains it this way: "The scribe responds correctly, but he cannot bring himself to say, 'the Samaritan.' The merciful person is simply called 'the one' (10:37). Jesus concludes their exchange by telling the scribe to emulate that neighbor, the Samaritan, in order to fulfill the command to love (10:37). Once again, the people of God are taught about true faith through an encounter with one outside and rejected by their culture."[4]

In the same way, we can learn a great deal about bighearted hospitality and loving our neighbors from those outside our culture. Because, unfortunately, Americans are not doing a good job with even the most basic dinner invitation, much less all-up-in-your-business care like the Samaritan demonstrated. In fact, the Billy Graham Center found that only one in ten immigrants has ever even been invited into the home of a U.S. citizen.[5] Christians have a biblical call to welcome the stranger, and only ten percent of immigrants have been invited into an American home! To my knowledge, the center didn't collect statistics on how many have been force-fed homemade lime concoctions for a cough, but I strongly suspect it's even less.

What is stopping us from opening up our homes, our lives, our hearts to the strangers in our midst? Are we dropping the ball on hospitality altogether, waiting for our farmhouse decor and colorful pineapple-and-steak kabob skills to be honed for perfect presentation? Are we too busy to work hospitality into our lives? Or are we afraid of saying the wrong things, doing the wrong things, cooking the wrong things? Too disconnected from those who are different from us to know where to start?

I'm afraid that welcoming the stranger may always be awkward. Encounters with strangers are a toss-up. You just never know what will happen. You might click instantly and have a new close friend. Or you might stick your foot in your mouth and have to apologize. Frankly, you may find yourself in new situations where you simply have no idea what's going on. Many years ago at a neighborhood barbecue, a young African American girl asked me to help fix her ponytail. I didn't know her, and as a white person, I didn't know much about black women's hair. But her request was simple, and I obliged. And then her hair fell out into my hands. I had no idea what to do with the weave I was now holding. Should I push it back into her ponytail somehow? Set it down somewhere? Or do what I did: stuff it into her jeans pocket and say, "Take that to your mom"?

If you take the risk to engage new people across cultures, it's inevitable mistakes will be made. One friend shared with me how she invited Muslim friends to a lunch meeting . . . in the middle of Ramadan, the month when Muslims fast from sunrise to sunset. She was embarrassed, but they graciously attended and participated in the conversation while still choosing to maintain their fast.

In my experience, there is enough grace for us all as we seek to engage across cultures. Denying hospitality for fear of making a mistake cannot be our default position when meeting someone new. The reality is that bighearted hospitality does not require the perfect timing, precise foods, or savvy conversation starters. Sometimes all it requires is a turkey sandwich.

* * *

Before my trip to Guatemala, Billy and I were sitting on the couch in my apartment, talking about our respective days at work, when he casually mentioned how he rarely ate lunch during the day. I was shocked and horrified. As a person who takes all meals very seriously, this revelation was beyond my comprehension. He was outside ten to twelve hours a day, working in roadside construction in Southern California. Without lunch? You do not want someone who's "hangry" operating a jackhammer, was all I could think. Despite the many indignities Billy had shared from his immigration experience, it was lunch that really got me riled up.

So I marched into my small kitchen and started making a sandwich. It was nothing fancy. Some smeared mayonnaise on whole wheat bread. A piece of cheese. I did hesitate ever so slightly about sharing my Trader Joe's cracked pepper turkey lunch meat. It was a personal delicacy I rarely allowed myself on my tight grocery budget. But then I felt bad about my proclivity toward self-preservation and selfishness, so I tossed on some meat and slid the sandwich into a baggie. I added an apple and some chips and returned to the living room, pushing the brown paper bag into his hands. It was a meager schoolboy's lunch for the next day, but it was something.

Months later, after Billy first told me he loved me, he reminded me of that moment. For me, it was a simple—maybe even pitiful—bagged lunch. But Billy experienced this offering as a deeply moving act of care, the kind of care he had rarely experienced since arriving in the United States. For him, it was a pioneering act of hospitality that unlocked a door to our deepening relationship.

The point of bighearted hospitality is not the act itself. It may be an invitation to tea, a potluck, backyard s'mores, or a multicourse meal with flair rivaling Martha Stewart's. Or it may be a cup of sweet coffee, a ride to the bus station, and a spoonful of homemade cough syrup. It may even look like bandages and gauze on the side of the road, a ride to the nearest clinic, and a room in which to recover.

Then again, it may simply be a turkey sandwich stuffed into a brown paper bag. No, the point of bighearted hospitality is to demonstrate our love for God by showing love to strangers. The specific action stems from the needs at our doorstep and a willingness to open our hands and offer everything to the version of God right in front of us. The stranger in our midst.

7

GARMENT OF DESTINY

*B*illy fidgeted on the couch, clearly trying to form his words carefully. "How was your day?" was what he came up with.

"Um, fine," I responded, waiting for the real reason he'd asked me to cancel our evening plans with friends. The air felt heavy with anticipation, but not in a good way.

"What's going on?" I asked.

He launched into a circuitous story, filled with awkward questions. "You know how I go to work every day? And I work for a guy named Anthony?"

"Uh-huh."

"Well, I work with other guys too. And most of us—well, really all of us—are undocumented. Pretty much everyone who works for the company."

"Okay."

He rambled on, his eyes dodging mine. "So . . . um . . . yeah. Today Anthony told me that he's having some trouble paying me. With my paperwork." Billy leaned back against the couch and closed his eyes. "Anthony asked if he could put you on the payroll instead."

"Wait. What?"

"He says a lot of the other guys do it. Their wives or girl-friends have valid socials, so they receive the checks from the company."

The Social Security Administration estimates that in 2010, 1.8 million of more than 10 million unauthorized immigrants "worked and used an SSN that did not match their name."[1] This practice has added complexity to the conversation about un-documented immigrants in the workplace. On the one hand, some consider this use of false information a prime example of fraudulent and criminal behavior. And when immigrants are caught using a Social Security number that belongs to some-one else, their misdemeanor "illegal entry" charges can be es-calated to a federal felony. In an NBC News report, columnist Bob Sullivan explains, "Prosecutors got in the habit of using federal identity theft laws to seek a mandatory two-year felony sentence enhancement for convicted suspects, and used that threat as bargaining tool to push suspects into plea bargains."[2] He goes on to note, however, that courts have been mixed in their support of this charge.

In fact, in 2015, Maria Eudofilia Arias—a wife, mother of three, and an undocumented immigrant from Ecuador—appealed her removal orders to the United States Court of Appeals for the Seventh Circuit. Immigrants can request dis-cretion from the Justice Department to lift deportation orders if they have not committed a "crime involving moral turpitude."[3] Arias's sole criminal conviction was because she used a false Social Security number to get a job.

The Board of Immigration Appeals had determined this *was* a crime involving moral turpitude and upheld her deportation orders. But the court of appeals disagreed. In the 2016 *Arias v. Lynch* decision, the court concluded,

It seems inconsistent with the terms "base, vile, or depraved" to hold that an unauthorized immigrant who uses a false social security number so that she can hold a job, pay taxes, and support her family would be guilty of a crime involving moral turpitude, while an unauthorized immigrant who is paid solely in cash under the table and does not pay any taxes would not necessarily be guilty of a crime involving moral turpitude. A rule that all crimes that involve any element of deception categorically involve moral turpitude would produce results at odds with the accepted definition of moral turpitude as conduct that is "inherently base, vile, or depraved."[4]

The legal ramifications of using a false Social Security number to gain employment remain in flux. On January 25, 2017, President Donald Trump signed an executive order that broadened the enforcement priorities of Homeland Security to include "removable aliens who have been convicted of any criminal offense; have been charged with any criminal offense, where such charge has not been resolved; have committed acts that constitute a chargeable criminal offense; [or] have engaged in fraud or willful misrepresentation in connection with any official matter or application before a governmental agency."[5] Advocates for immigrants worry that this broad language— which includes people who've been convicted of a crime, people who have been charged with a crime (but not convicted), or anyone whom the Department of Homeland Security *thinks* has committed a crime—essentially makes all undocumented immigrants top priority for deportation. The inclusion of "willful misrepresentation" could make it more likely that using a false Social Security number would be an infraction leading to deportation priority.

But there is another government agency that has more ambiguous feelings about the 1.8 million immigrants using false

Social Security numbers: the Internal Revenue Service. IRS commissioner John Koskinen was questioned during a session of the Senate Finance Committee after a look at agency procedures suggested the IRS was processing false W-2 information and ignoring notifications from the Social Security Administration when names and Social Security numbers didn't match. Koskinen's response, as quoted in the *Washington Examiner*, was, "'What happens in these situations is someone is using a Social Security number to get a job, but they're filing their tax return with their [taxpayer identification number].' What that means, he said, is that 'they are undocumented aliens. . . . They're paying taxes. It's in everybody's interest to have them pay the taxes they owe.'"[6]

The Social Security Administration documents this same kind of positive contribution. They found that undocumented immigrants paid $13 billion in 2010 payroll taxes into Social Security, but only collected about $1 billion in benefit payments. The Social Security office notes, "Thus, we estimate that earnings by unauthorized immigrants result in a net positive effect on Social Security financial status generally, and that this effect contributed roughly $12 billion to the cash flow of the program for 2010. We estimate that future years will experience a continuation of this positive impact on the trust funds."[7]

While the request from Billy's boss may have benefited the IRS and the Social Security Administration, I sat on the couch in silence. I gave my mind a moment to wrap itself around the possible ramifications for Billy and me. As if lost in a corn maze, my frenzied thoughts scurried down every path in rapid succession. How will this affect my taxes? What are the potential legal consequences? This is wrong! Absolutely not! But what other options does Billy have? How could this decision affect our future? Our immigration system is outdated and dysfunctional.

Someone is asking me to use my privilege to stand in the gap for him. How serious am I about my commitment to justice?

Billy spoke with emotion. "I hate to ask you this. I don't want to ask you this. I don't know what to do. I don't want to lose my job, but I don't want you to be affected."

I nodded. We sat in silence, holding hands.

* * *

"We are tied together in the single garment of destiny, caught in an inescapable network of mutuality," said Martin Luther King Jr. in a now famous quotation. "And whatever affects one directly affects all indirectly. For some strange reason I can never be what I ought to be until you are what you ought to be. . . . This is the way God's universe is made; this is the way it is structured."[8]

The interconnectedness of society was stark for me in that moment on the couch. Immigration enforcement and the challenges of being undocumented were no longer just "Billy's issues." As our connection deepened, the frayed edges of the immigration system were now touching me as well.

I had already noticed the ways our relationship was changing me, sharpening my senses and adjusting the lens on my worldview. My cheeks grew warm when I heard people speak about immigrants in demeaning or uninformed ways. Now that I knew Billy, when I encountered immigrant families through my job, I picked up on clues about who was undocumented that I would have previously missed. And when the Immigration Reform Act of 2007 was working its way through Capitol Hill, I was paying attention. Had I not been dating an immigrant, I likely wouldn't have known anything about it.

The bill had been introduced to the Senate in early May 2007 and was being touted as a compromise with hopes of attracting enough congressional support to be enacted. The legislation included provisions for increased border security and workplace enforcement, along with opportunities for legal status adjustment for current undocumented immigrants, which heartened Billy and his coworkers. Spanish-language radio stations tracked the life of the bill, and Billy provided me with near-daily updates on its progress.

President George W. Bush worked to solicit support for the bill, which he hoped would address the major issues facing the outdated immigration system. But debate raged in Congress. The challenge with compromises is that everyone is opposing something. In the end, the bill died in the Senate in June 2007. With the 2008 elections on the horizon, Congress was unlikely to touch the risky political topic for a while.[9]

But for those of us who loved someone directly affected by the bill's demise, it was devastating. Billy called me from the job site. "No one feels like working," he told me. "Everyone is just really sad."

* * *

When we follow God's call to build bridges across society's divides, our perspectives begin to shift ever so slightly. Without even trying to, we learn to weep with those who mourn and rejoice with those who celebrate (Romans 12:15). Suddenly, those issues that affect our brothers and sisters are part of our own lives. A neighbor shares that she lost her much-needed job because her son has asthma and the mix of unreliable public transportation and scattershot doctor's appointments caused her to miss too much work—and suddenly we are very interested in job opportunities, public transit funding, and Medicaid. When one of the very causes of the increased cases of asthma in urban areas is actually a side effect of massive highways subsidizing commuters' desire for private transit, we become even more passionate about the need for clean energy and sustainable transportation options. When neighbors who do not have access to a car are required to travel three hours round-trip to access fresh produce, we become passionate about "food deserts" and finding sustainable retail options that provide fresh fruits and vegetables in the community.

And when the man I loved and his coworkers lamented the death of a bill that sought to invite them out of the shadows and to allow them full participation in the place they called home, I discovered a tiny seed of passion for immigration reform germinating in my heart.

But when we are isolated from those experiencing the intensity of injustice, our urgency is often lacking. Martin Luther King Jr. illuminates this truth in his famous *Letter from Birmingham Jail.* He was responding to a group of white Alabama pastors who criticized the methods of the civil rights movement. They had made a call for unity and negotiation without addressing the underlying reality that had created the movement's direct action responses. King wrote, "You are exactly right in your call for negotiation. Indeed, this is the purpose of direct action. Nonviolent direct action seeks to create such a crisis and establish such creative tension that a community that has consistently refused to negotiate is forced to confront the issue. It seeks so to dramatize the issue that it can no longer be ignored."[10]

Important issues affecting vulnerable people are still largely being ignored. But the line between engaging and dismissing injustice feels blurrier, I believe, in our world of social media, push notifications, and the twenty-four-hour news cycle. Many of us are bombarded by the heartbreak of the day as passions for worldwide injustices swell and recede online. As if we were standing in the surf, we pay attention as issues roll in and bury our feet. But then, just as quickly, they pull back out into the vast ocean, where we can no longer see the specific wave that touched us. As hard as it may be to admit, it can be difficult to care beyond the few seconds the story flashes on the screen or the article zooms past on our phones. We might double-tap an Instagram photo of a young boy rescued from ISIL in Syria, share a powerful article on Facebook, or hashtag our favorite Twitter causes—before being immediately called back to our "real life," which too often is very disconnected from these issues of the day.

Relationships are key for sustaining justice work long-term. When we are in relationship with those most affected by the news, we cannot escape the real consequences of executive orders and Supreme Court rulings. Instead of experiencing apathy or justice fatigue, we are sustained by our relationships in the long and valuable work toward justice. We fall to our knees, calling out to El Roi, the God who sees. We pray by name for those we know who are suffering abuse and injustice, who live in fear and terror. We do not need reminders to seek God's face on behalf of the poor and the mistreated, because they are our friends. We cannot *not* pray for them and against the systems that hold them captive.

This committed solidarity requires that our relationships across cultures move past any one-way dynamics of giver and receiver and into true mutuality and friendship. There is a place for acts of service. A refugee needs assistance renting an apartment, so we go with him to help translate and navigate the unfamiliar system. An exchange student has nowhere to go for the holidays, so we invite her over to share our turkey and mashed potatoes. A mother cannot read her child's homework, so we set up a tutoring program to help young children succeed in school and offer support to struggling parents. These tangible connections and resources are valuable. But as we step across race, culture, class, and other societal barriers, we must recognize these interactions as first steps—on-ramps to building authentic relationships.

To deepen our friendships may require a level of intention that stretches us. Many of our interactions lack any official declaration or shared purpose. Romantic relationships like the one Billy and I were developing have the benefit of some type of DTR ("define the relationship") conversation. Where is this going? What future do we have? Do you like me as much as I like you? Could this work? In these relationships, there are moments of vulnerability that transition a relationship to "the next level." But when we consider how to go deeper in our friendships, the biblical story of Ruth's undying solidarity with her mother-in-law Naomi demonstrates an intentionality that can be a model for our relationships across various lines.

Naomi, like so many immigrants today, had left her home because she and her husband were unable to feed their family because of famine (Ruth 1:1). She stayed in the land of Moab for more than a decade, even after her husband died, and eventually her two sons passed away as well. She had lost everyone she came with and the very people she had sought to care and provide for. More than once, Naomi laments that the Lord has come against her (Ruth 1:13, 20-21). She decides to return to her homeland in Bethlehem, and she attempts to send her daughters-in-law away, back to their own homes. But Ruth launches into a DTR conversation that leaves no room for doubt about whom she stands with.

> "Do not urge me to leave you or to return from following you. For where you go I will go, and where you lodge I will lodge.

Your people shall be my people, and your God my God. Where you die I will die, and there will I be buried. May the Lord do so to me and more also if anything but death parts me from you." And when Naomi saw that she was determined to go with her, she said no more. (Ruth 1:16-18)

These women are separated by age, religion, and nationality, but they are committed to each other for life. Ruth doesn't say, "Well, you seem like you will need a lot of help, so I'm going to go with you to get you set up and settled in before I head back to my real life." She lets Naomi know in no uncertain terms that she is in it. Till death do them part. Solidarity.

Because of their shared life, what affects one has consequences for the other. Ruth goes out into the fields and collects grain that feeds them both. Then Naomi advises her on how to attract Boaz and secure their future. And when Ruth and Boaz have a son, Naomi, now the former mother-in-law, becomes his nurse (Ruth 4:16). These two women each experience the hardships of being a foreigner in the other's land. But they are blessed to walk alongside each other throughout their lives, serving and supporting one another.

* * *

True relationships are mutual. There is give and take. Vulnerability is shared, and friendship deepens organically. Everyday moments of wrangling kids at the park, watching international soccer games on TV, and chatting over the stove open into raucous laughter or free-flowing tears. These are the real moments on which friendships are built.

When we develop cross-cultural relationships, we are also walking into a bigger and ongoing story of unique groups of people experiencing the world. Cultural and racial differences are real and should not be ignored. But these barriers should also not be elevated in such ways as to assume that we cannot be true friends. There can be damaging interactions when we swing too far in either direction.

Some assume that we are all the same and any differences are simply superficial. While that perspective may sound delightful and kumbaya-y, it often glosses over the ways history influences the present and real difference in lived experiences. We cannot be in authentic relationship with someone different from us if we cannot acknowledge that, while another's experience in the world may be different than our own, it is just as true. In *Fear of the Other*, William Willimon writes, "We cannot have community without recognition of the reality of deeply different history and experience that must be honored if another is to be understood in all of his or her delightful, God-given difference."[11] Too often, people in positions of privilege try to explain away what they perceive as anomalies without recognizing the ways systematic racism and injustice are at work in the world.

Billy's experience in the United States was squarely shaped by an outdated immigration system, and it was easy for me to forget that fact. For example, I loved to dance, and I often wanted to go out in the evenings to dance. Billy always resisted. While his hesitation was certainly because he didn't like to dance, he also admitted that going out late at night, when police were more likely to be in the streets and patrolling for drunk drivers, made him very nervous as an undocumented immigrant. As a matter of safety, he tried to stay away from all nightlife. I couldn't dismiss his legitimate concern, though it was new to me.

On the other hand, it's possible to become so focused on cultural and other differences in ways that can lead only to wider gaps and isolation. Our role as bridge builders is to identify the strength of our common humanity and our similarities of experience and interests to serve as the foundation for an authentic relationship. Maybe your parents immigrated to the United States from a country I've never known, but we both love basketball and can enjoy watching the NBA Finals together. Maybe we come from different race and class backgrounds, but we're both recently married and can share conversations about navigating the unique bonds of marriage.

Our common humanity is ready and waiting to lay a foundation for authentic connection, but we must be clear that we see the humanity in the other in every moment. When someone becomes a service project, the relationship lacks a deeper authenticity. Billy and I may have come from different countries and may have spoken different first languages, but we connected over our shared sense of humor, adventurous spirits, and affinity for movies about magicians. When we place dignity at the center of our friendships, seeing and appreciating the other as made in the image of God, we can enter into mutual, loving relationships.

And this invitation can lead us down a path toward solidarity and a life enriched by the experiences and perspectives of another. Then, when the headlines fly past, we freeze when we see those we love caught in the middle of suffering, injustice, and pain. We cannot look away, and we feel compelled to engage. When those we love are being pushed down, we do what we can to lift the beam pressing against their chests.

Our world is full of heartbreak. Sometimes it's enough to make me want to disconnect from everything and retreat into my cheery little life. But I am convinced that the fracturing of the world deepens our need for relationships that cross boundaries of race, ethnicity, religion, and socioeconomic status.

These real-life friendships may draw us into suffering that we could have previously ignored, but they will also guide us into new ways to love God and love people.

As Billy and I considered Anthony's request, we were both already thinking of marriage. While the situation felt urgent, we had a long-term plan we didn't want to jeopardize. So we agreed not to respond. Thankfully, Anthony never brought up the conversation again. And Billy continued to be paid.

Then, a few weeks later, Billy was fidgeting again. He was hemming and hawing and trying to form sentences about how much he loved me. He got down on one knee and asked me to marry him.

I immediately said yes, and I couldn't wait to start life together with this man I had come to love so deeply. We did not yet know how this commitment—and Billy's immigration status—could affect me and our future together. Like Ruth, I was all in.

8

MOUNTAINS OF PAPERWORK

A white sign with blue letters identified the lawyer's office in the small business strip. Billy searched for parking while I clutched our paperwork. My U.S. passport, Billy's two Guatemalan ones. His Guatemalan ID card. His expired driver's license from the State of California from when his visa was valid. I shuffled them all into a neat pile and held on tightly. Then I released them slightly. I didn't want them to crumple or get wet from my sweaty hands.

Only a few nights before, Billy and I had gotten engaged. Marrying Billy seemed like the most natural thing in the world to me. We already felt like family, and I was ready to make it official. We set a date only ten weeks away, which kicked the wedding planning into high gear. I was a difficult bride, mostly because I was hopelessly uninterested in wedding colors and flower arrangements. I simply wanted to go to the beach with my love, read a good book in the sand, and occasionally shout, "We're getting married!" over the sound of the ocean.

The short engagement worked in my favor. There was a light at the end of the tunnel for conversations about bridesmaid dresses and centerpieces, and we were able to focus on life after the wedding at the same time. We signed a lease on our future apartment and started dreaming about weeknight dinners at home, hosting friends and family, and generally building life together as a couple. I couldn't wait. Another benefit of the quick turnaround was knowing a forthcoming wedding would also push along Billy's immigration process. I worried that if he were detained or deported, our lives would get much more complicated. The sooner we could resolve his status issues, the better.

Our plan was to ask the lawyer about a fiancé visa. We'd heard that once engaged, we could apply for this type of visa, which would offer Billy some immediate security until we were married and could go through the official process for a green card. Still, it felt unnerving. What if we were wrong and the lawyer said we didn't have any options? We were *pretty* sure my citizenship would allow me to apply for Billy, but we'd also heard that in some cases, it didn't always work out. Our knowledge base was built mostly out of crowdsourced rumors. Since there were very few people we could open up to about our situation, we'd gleaned information from scattered media reports, the Internet, and stories from trusted friends about people *they* knew who knew someone who knew someone who had experienced something similar. But since visiting a lawyer while dating had seemed utterly ridiculous, this post-engagement meeting was our first step into the truth of our future together. And in reality, I didn't know what to expect.

We walked down the three cement stairs to the low-level storefront shops and found the office. A bell chimed when we opened the door to the small waiting room. Billy spoke in Spanish with the receptionist while I took a seat on a padded folding chair. The place was clean and bright. It reminded me of the travel agency on *The Truman Show*, eerily quiet and decorated with frightening posters about your rights and dangerous situations to avoid. A heavyset, dark-skinned Latino man sat along the wall adjacent to me. A woman with long black hair, who I assumed to be his wife or girlfriend, sat next to him, a young child on her lap. I smiled and waved at the little girl. She buried her face in her mother's chest. I wondered about their story. Were they a mixed-status couple like us? Were they undocumented parents with a U.S.-born daughter? I felt conspicuous and out of place, almost as if I were trespassing on a sacred place where vulnerable families could come for safety. I didn't want to stare or make others feel uncomfortable. So when Billy sat down next to me, I turned my attention to him.

"Guillermo?" The lawyer stuck his head out of his office, calling Billy by his full name. We scurried inside, gripping our paperwork, and sat down next to each other.

"We're engaged!" we announced. The lawyer, Mateo, congratulated us. But his kind words quickly shifted to the business at hand. Mostly he asked Billy questions in Spanish. I tried to keep up. When did you come? How did you come? How long have you been here? What do you do for work? The lawyer reached out for documents, and I handed him the pile of IDs and passports.

He skimmed through them in silence while we waited. I looked at Billy, raising my eyebrows and sneaking in a faint shrug. What was happening? He nodded but turned his attention back to Mateo. Nothing.

We waited. This wasn't going exactly how I'd expected. I had hoped the meeting would be cut and dried. I was a U.S. citizen, Billy was my fiancé, and we wanted a fiancé visa. Sign, dot, cross, go get ice cream.

Mateo looked up. "I think the best thing . . ." he said in Spanish. My mind tried to translate as he spoke. "The best thing is to go ahead and get married. And then come back to see me after you're officially husband and wife." Billy was answering, but I was confused. Had I understood correctly? I nudged Billy's knee.

When Mateo looked down at one of the papers, I leaned over to Billy and mumbled, "Fiancé visa?" Billy nodded in acknowledgment and said something to Mateo in Spanish. All I could make out was Billy's repetition of *visa de comprometido*: "fiancé visa." Mateo cocked his head to the side and let out a discouraging "Ehhh."

He pondered a moment before declaring no, it wasn't an option. I didn't know why not. Mateo again encouraged us to return once the marriage was official and legal, and promised we'd go from there. There were some forms we'd need to complete, some fees we'd need to pay, but it should be pretty straightforward once we were married.

Suddenly, Mateo rifled through the cards and papers and passports and retrieved Billy's current Guatemalan passport. He flipped through the pages and found the stamp from his most recent arrival to the States. I heard him ask Billy a question. I couldn't grasp the translation, but the tone had changed. He sounded grave. Billy answered with an "Um . . ." while he, too, shuffled through more of the papers we'd stuck neatly inside a folder.

"No sé," I heard him answer. I don't know. The only thing *I* was sure of was the confusion on Billy's face. I stared at him, completely lost.

I felt so vulnerable. I perched on the edge of my seat, back straight and knees bouncing, while my eyes jumped frantically between my fiancé and my lawyer. The future swirled around me, but I couldn't follow the conversation. I could read the body language—concern, confusion, disappointment—but

I couldn't decode the words. No one was asking for the location of the bathroom or a hotel, so my college Spanish was failing me. The sudden change of the room's tone had flooded my body with stress, and my mind couldn't concentrate. I gave up. Instead, I sat there smiling and fidgeting, tapping Billy ever so slightly every few minutes. But he never broke eye contact with Mateo while quietly gesturing for me to hold on.

Not knowing what's going on is quite possibly one of the most maddening feelings in the world. I think about the day-to-day experience of immigrants in this country who may be learning English but are still most comfortable in their native tongue. I think of parents who sit in meetings with school administrators and program leaders, and I empathize with that unsteady feeling of trying to translate important information with developing bilingual skills. I wonder about encounters with police, medical professionals, and supervisors, and all the language challenges and stresses that make up a life of living across cultures. I know how some of these incidents can bring humor. Billy loved it when I decided to order fruit in Spanish from a local street vendor and accidentally requested cocaine instead of coconut. As the fruit seller's eyes widened, Billy immediately jumped in to clarify. But sitting in lawyer's office, I also recognized how these confusions could bring real frustration and fear.

Living in a country that doesn't share your first language is an expected hurdle for many immigrants. But I empathized with that vulnerability and uncertainty in a new, deeper way as I listened to Billy and our lawyer rapidly exchange questions and confused responses while I watched them shuffle papers.

I was used to being independent, and I was comfortable meeting new people, gathering information, and asking questions. But they held my future in a language that I couldn't unlock. I would have to wait to find out the truth until someone decided to include me.

* * *

Finally, mercifully, Billy turned to me. "It seems like I'm missing a piece of paper they gave me when I entered the U.S." I stared back at him blankly. "It's a form I guess I filled out when I arrived, and the government keeps half, and I was supposed to keep the other half. But I don't have it."

"Okay?" I responded, looking back and forth between Billy and Mateo.

Mateo picked up in English. "It's called an I-94, and they usually staple the second half into your passport when you enter. Then, when you leave, Customs rips it off and keeps it. It signifies that you entered legally and then exited properly. But Billy's is missing."

Billy and I both looked at him, unsure of the implication. He continued, "Basically, because it's gone, it looks like Billy left the country."

"But I'm here." Billy laughed at the incongruity.

"Yes," Mateo answered. "According to your paperwork, you entered the country legally with your Guatemalan passport and a ten-year U.S. tourist visa. But then you left. And the fact that you are here without an I-94 means—*solely according to your paperwork*—you then reentered the country illegally after you left."

"Even though I have a valid visa?" Billy asked.

"Yes," Mateo confirmed. "It doesn't make any sense why you would enter the country illegally when you have a visa, but that's the story your paperwork tells."

"What does that mean?" I piped up.

"It means you may not be able to adjust your status from here in the U.S.," Mateo said. "After you get married, you may need to move to Guatemala and apply for legal residence from his home country. That process could be as short as three months or could take as long as ten years. It's not guaranteed, but he *should* qualify once you go through that procedure."

What? How, in the course of ten minutes, did our legal options go from "a few forms and some fees" to "ten years living abroad" and "it may or may not work out"? I was stunned.

This shift rattled my assumption that simply "marrying a U.S. citizen" would be a simple and clear process. As the American Immigration Council observes, "Most Americans take it for granted that marriage to a U.S. citizen and other family relationships entitle an immigrant to permanent residence (a green card), but there are barriers that often prevent or delay these family members from becoming lawful permanent residents, even if they are already in the United States."[1] Billy held a passport, had a valid visa, and had purchased a plane ticket to fly into the States. Up until he lost his I-94, these criteria—coupled with the facts that he'd had zero run-ins with law enforcement and I made an income the government determined sufficient to support us both without him drawing on public benefits—made it possible for him to adjust his status through a relatively straightforward process and without leaving the country.

But the paperwork story that he had entered the country illegally had changed the game. Billy risked being barred from the country for ten years. The three- and ten-year bars are some of the biggest repercussions for undocumented immigrants who marry U.S. citizens. They are punitive measures that say those who have lived illegally in the States for less than a year are barred from returning for three years. Those who have stayed without authorization in the country for more than a year cannot return for ten years.[2]

While a country has the right to impose consequences for violating its laws, these bars helped me understand why some undocumented immigrants who may be eligible for adjustment because of marriage to a U.S. citizen choose not to begin the process. Many people who qualify for green cards are caught in a catch-22, says the American Immigration Council. "Under current law they must leave the United States to apply for their green card abroad, but as soon as they depart, they are immediately barred from reentering the country for a period of time."[3] As Mateo laid out our options, Billy and I realized that we, too, were now squeezed between this rock and hard place. Billy's missing paperwork required us to apply from outside the country. But if we chose to leave, he would risk being denied entry for up to ten years.

What would my life look like for ten years in Guatemala? I wondered. Was I up for that? When Billy's boss had asked to use my Social Security number, we had been able to avoid giving an answer. But if we wanted to adjust Billy's status, we were going to have to face whatever came once we were married. And I wouldn't know what that would be until after I said "I do."

Self-preservation peeked in and whispered in my ear. Was this a good idea? Did I love Billy so much that I was willing to suffer personal risk because of our relationship? The reality was he might be barred from the United States for ten years. In order to be with him, I'd essentially be evicted as well. I thought I was prepared for marital sacrifices like remembering to put the cap back on the toothpaste tube or going to the movie theater for every film in the *Transformers* franchise. Was this more than I had bargained for?

In his book *Break Open the Sky*, Stephan Bauman, the former president of World Relief, writes, "We are perplexed, torn between principle and what seems practical, between love and safety, and between faith and fear."[4] I valued standing in solidarity with immigrants harmed by an outdated immigration system, but I was also afraid to lose something in the process. I wanted to be engaged in the world and to stand up for justice, but with the assurance that I could retreat to safety whenever the flames got too hot. Mateo's declaration of our potential exile would require me to step outside the immunity of my citizenship and tie my fate to someone who, in this situation, didn't have access to the same privileges that I had. Did I have the strength to do that? Could I trust God was leading us down this path together, wherever it might lead?

When Jesus tells his disciples that he is headed toward suffering and death before being raised from the dead, they have strong reactions. "Peter took him aside and began to rebuke him, saying, 'Far be it from you, Lord! This shall never happen to you'" (Matthew 16:22). Only a few verses prior, Peter had declared that Jesus was the Christ, Son of the living God (verse 16). Peter was a committed follower of Jesus, and he couldn't fathom that God's Son would suffer in the way he'd described. Jesus' response leaves no room for doubt.

> He turned and said to Peter, "Get behind me, Satan! You are a hindrance to me. For you are not setting your mind on the things of God, but on the things of man."
>
> Then Jesus told his disciples, "If anyone would come after me, let him deny himself and take up his cross and follow me. For whoever would save his life will lose it, but whoever loses his life for my sake will find it. For what will it profit a man if he gains the whole world and forfeits his soul? Or what shall a man give in return for his soul?" (Matthew 16:23-26)

For Billy and me, faith was foundational to our relationship. We had committed our lives to Jesus long before we met each other. I had often heard in church that following Jesus would mean sacrifice, but had I ever really experienced it? Bauman writes, "When we are afraid, we are more likely to compromise what's most important to us—our convictions about faith, character, or even the nature of truth. We are especially susceptible when we are offered some form of real or perceived security in exchange for compromising our faith."[5]

I knew I could walk away and my friends and family would understand. Our future together was uncertain and risky. But I loved Billy, and I knew that decision would cost me even more than my relationship with him. I would be choosing my own comfort and security over standing alongside someone I loved in the midst of struggle. Was I willing to make that trade-off?

In the 2017 movie *Wonder Woman*, Diana (Wonder Woman) learns that the world of men is entrenched in a terrible war. She is poised to leave the safety of her home with the Amazons to fight and help when her mother, Queen Hippolyta, tells her, "If you choose to leave, you may never return." Diana responds, "Who will I be if I stay?" I wrestled with the reverse question: Who will I be if I leave?

* * *

"Like I said," Mateo announced, trying to sound cheerful after delivering this devastating premarital news. "Go ahead and get married. Come back to see me, and we'll start the process. You have options, better than many couples I work with. You saw that family in the waiting area?"

He nodded toward the entrance. "They have no chance. But they keep coming to me to try to work it out. I have to keep telling them they have no options. You?" he paused. "You have options." I tried to be comforted by these words, but the uncertainty of our future together loomed over us as we stepped back out into the sunny afternoon.

9

CELEBRATION

"But how will people know who the groom is?" Billy deadpanned, a desperate look on his face.

I laughed. "You're joking, right?"

"No," he countered. "If the groomsmen and I are all wearing the same thing, no one will know who is getting married!"

I could only shake my head. Our ten-week engagement had been a whirl of back-to-back conversations and decisions. Where would we host the reception? What color flowers? How many cakes? I had answered that one easily: "As many as possible!" I'd bypassed all the traditional wedding towers and told the caterer I wanted carrot cake, chocolate cake, strawberry cake, and any other kind of cake she suggested. I may have been phoning in the rest of our wedding details, but I took dessert very seriously.

"Fine. How about you wear a jacket? The groomsmen can wear dress shirts and slacks, but you can add a jacket. That'll help everyone know it's your special day," I suggested with only a hint of mockery.

"That sounds good," Billy conceded. "And pinstripes. They can wear black, but mine will have stripes." Oh, for the love.

But I wasn't going to argue about wedding favors or playlists or pinstripes. The day after our meeting with the lawyer, he'd called to tell us it was possible to apply for a replacement I-94. Suddenly, with the completion of a short application and a cashier's check for a couple hundred dollars, we would again find ourselves in the status of "best-case scenario." Once married, we could apply from the United States to adjust Billy's status. He told us the process would cost a couple thousand of dollars but that everything should be in order in about six months.

Having recently faced the possibility of a ten-year relocation to a country I'd only visited once, I thought pinstripes were barely worth mentioning. I leaned over and kissed Billy. I was happy, and I simply wanted to celebrate with the people we loved.

But it turned out even that hope was becoming more complicated. Billy had asked his brother and his friend Juan, one of the original instigators of our relationship, to be his groomsmen. I complained about his short list, bemoaning that I felt so limited at two bridesmaids. Billy apologized and admitted he had several other friends, including his former bandmates, who he'd hoped would stand with him. But these guys had already come to terms with the fact that getting U.S. visas would be too challenging. They congratulated him over the phone but wouldn't be able to come to the ceremony.

Billy's parents, on the other hand, had immediately applied for tourist visas to attend. Nonimmigrant arrivals to the United States have different options than the "blood, sweat, and tears" avenues for immigrant visas. In fact, there are more than twenty unique classifications for nonimmigrant visas, including tourism, business travel, exchange visitors (for private-sector cultural exchange such as scholars, au pairs, interns, and so on), students, and "specialty workers," who are highly skilled professionals in fields like engineering, technology, medicine, and higher education.[1] The United States also has a visa waiver program that allows business or tourist travelers from thirty-eight countries to enter the States for ninety days or less without a visa. Some of the countries participating in this program include Australia, Chile, Denmark, Finland, France, Germany, Ireland, Italy, Japan, New Zealand, Norway, South Korea, and Spain. The U.S. Department of State notes on its website there is a prohibition if "citizens of one of these countries are also a national of Iraq, Iran, Syria, or Sudan."[2]

For Cuty and Lucky, the prerequisites to receive a travel visa were somewhat vague. According to Section 214(b) of the U.S. Immigration and Nationality Act, the government assumes that any visa applicant is planning to immigrate. Therefore, the burden is on the visa applicant to overcome this legal presumption and prove that they really won't be immigrating—just visiting—and therefore qualify for a nonimmigrant visa.[3] One website offers examples of how to do this, suggesting that the visa applicant demonstrate that the purpose of the trip is a temporary visit, the plan is specific and time-bound, that all expenses while in the country have been accounted for and covered, and that the visitor owns a residence outside the States and has additional economic and social ties which support the case for a temporary visit only.[4] Billy's parents seemed to meet all these requirements, so we submitted their applications, along with the application fees of $160 each, which translated to more than 2,300 total quetzales in Guatemalan currency.

* * *

My cell phone rang while I was at work. I picked it up and closed my office door. "My mom called," Billy told me, his voice small and quiet. "She and my dad were denied visas for the wedding."

I sat silently for a moment, stunned. "What?" I finally asked. "But they met all the requirements!"

"I know," came the barely audible reply.

I was dumbstruck. I knew Billy had violated immigration laws, so the process with the lawyers and fees and paperwork was a consequence of that decision. But Cuty and Lucky were trying to do things "the right way." In my mind, it was all very simple. Billy and I were having a wedding. We wanted the parents of the groom to attend. They applied for the appropriate visa and met all the requirements. Bada bing! Bada boom! Thank you for our tourist visas!

Billy told me his mom was crying, distressed by this devastating news. Lucky—the woman who had welcomed me into her country, kissed my cheeks, and served me coffee with *champurradas*—was not welcome in my homeland. She was being denied entry to attend one of the major life events in a family. She would miss her baby son's wedding.

But Cuty and Lucky were not ready to give up. They hadn't been given a clear explanation for their denial, and the parting words of the immigration agent had essentially been "Better luck next time!" So they tried again, forking over another $160 each to the U.S. embassy, waiting for a capricious decision, the results of which we could not reasonably guess.

They were denied a second time, and were given another cheery encouragement to apply yet again. With payments to the U.S. government already more than $600 and no clear hope that trying again would be effective, Billy's parents decided not to do so. We tucked the sorrow in our hearts and kept looking ahead toward our wedding. Even as Billy's guest list dwindled, we tried to stay focused on the jubilee of our marriage.

* * *

Celebration is a wonderfully biblical concept. In his book on spiritual disciplines, *The Life You've Always Wanted*, John Ortberg has a chapter titled "A 'Dee Dah Day': The Practice of Celebration." I love the framing of celebration as a spiritual discipline. Ortberg writes, "When we celebrate, we exercise our ability to see and feel goodness in the simplest gifts of God. We are able to take delight today in something we wouldn't have even noticed yesterday. Our capacity for joy increases."[5]

Could a discipline of celebration create sacred space to notice God's lavish love? Could it provide respite and balance amid suffering and sorrow?

Most of us are familiar with celebration at the end of a hard-fought journey: the basketball banquet, the graduation party, the welcome home bash. In Luke 15, we watch the father in the parable of the prodigal son throw a huge feast to embrace the return of his boy. He says to his servants, "Bring quickly the best robe, and put it on him, and put a ring on his hand, and shoes on his feet. And bring the fattened calf and kill it, and let us eat and celebrate. For this my son was dead, and is alive again; he was lost, and is found" (Luke 15:22-24). He is welcoming his son home at the end of a difficult absence. Or so it seems.

For the older brother in the story, though, the party is out of sync. The prodigal brother did not do things "the right way," and it seems his wastefulness and irresponsibility is being honored. Meanwhile, the older brother has been waiting in the wings for his own party. The father reminds him that he could have celebrated at any time because everything he has also belongs to the son (verse 31). Ortberg writes, "The psalmist says, '*This* is the day the Lord has made; let us rejoice and be glad in *it*.' He doesn't say, 'Yesterday was God's day—how happy I was then.' Nor does he say, 'Tomorrow will be the great day—I'll just endure until then.' *This* day, with all its shortcomings, is the great Dee Dah Day." As Ortberg goes on to note, "We all live with the illusion that joy will come someday when conditions change."[6]

It is impossible to disentangle beauty from pain, joy from suffering, and celebration from sorrow. For so many people in the world, sorrow and suffering are inescapable, and yet . . . "And yet": here is a beautiful conjunction that God offers us. And yet celebration exists! It is a true testament to the resilience of people and the faithfulness of God that the suffering of this world does not shut down the block parties.

In the parable of the prodigal son, the father throws a welcome home bash for his lost son. At the same time, though, he experiences painful tension with another son who has been by his side but never really there. I imagine the father returning to the music and the party, genuinely delighted to watch his younger son doing the electric slide on the dance floor. I imagine him quickly dabbing at the tears at the corner of his eye, too, as he considers the loss of his other son.

* * *

Even as Billy and I tried to maintain good attitudes, our immigration situation continued to rear its ugly head at the least expected moments. Friends told us they'd heard a rumor that California was passing a law that would require a Social Security number to obtain a marriage license. We considered focusing on the religious ceremony and dealing with the legal marriage later—except we knew how important that legal marriage certificate was to our future. Billy gently suggested we dart off to Las Vegas for a quick, legal marriage before the big day. But while I was flexible on the pinstripes, I struggled to greet Elvis with the same kind of plucky good nature. Then, as quickly as our fears arose, we learned the rumor was untrue and we could get married in California—without Elvis—after all.

A bigger concern, however, was jogging steadily alongside our wedding planning, and it had more significant consequences for our future. Billy's paycheck was late. The boss had apologized for the inconvenience, assured the guys that the money would be there the next day. The next day, an excuse followed. On day three, a plea for patience. Guys began abandoning the job site. Billy didn't know what to do. He was the on-site supervisor, but he couldn't fault his guys for picking up other work until they got their checks. He decided to stick with it. After all, the company already owed him two weeks' worth of pay. If he walked away now, he might lose it. So he hoped for the best and kept showing up for work.

Before long, Billy was the only one left, working alone with a shovel, trying to do the work of an entire crew while inwardly panicking about his new—and apparently volunteer—position bringing faster Internet speed to homes in Southern California.

We were shopping for my rehearsal dinner dress when Billy received a phone call. He wandered away from me as I pushed through crowded hangers. I held up a blue floral print for inspection. Then I heard Billy's voice rising. Spanish flew through the air, and though I couldn't discern the words, I could tell he was frustrated. But he wasn't the only one. His voice softened as he tried to calm the person on the other end of the line. He was polite and patient, but definitive. He hung up and walked back into the women's dress department.

I pushed the hanger back onto the rack. "Who on earth was that?"

"It was the wife of one of my guys," he said. "She is furious. I picked up the phone, and she just started screaming at me, demanding her husband's paycheck." He shook his head. "She doesn't believe me that I'm not getting paid either. She can't understand why I'm still showing up to work. She's telling me she's going to sue."

He broke eye contact with me and stared vaguely across the store. "It's so sad. They know as well as I do that none of us are going to even report this, let alone sue anybody. We're all undocumented. We're just going to find new jobs and try to let it go."

Los Angeles has been called the "wage theft capital of the country," given the commonplace nature of wage violations, including denied overtime pay, required "off the clock" work, stolen tips, and unpaid wages.[7] A 2010 report from the Institute for Research on Labor and Employment estimated that more than six hundred thousand Los Angeles County workers experience at least one wage violation in a given week. In that county alone, "front-line workers in low-wage industries lose more than $26.2 million *per week* as a result of employment and labor law violations."[8] A 2014 report from the Economic Policy Institute puts wage theft nationwide at an estimated $50 billion annually.[9] To put that number in perspective, it may be helpful to note that in 2012, all the robberies (including bank, home, gas station, and street robberies) and car thefts in the nation amounted to less than $14 billion in losses.[10]

These numbers are difficult to pin down, however, because so many vulnerable workers in low-wage positions do not report wage theft. And it's understandable. In addition to concerns about immigration status for some employees, the benefits of pursuing action in these cases are minimal. In a report for the National Employment Law Project and UCLA Labor Center, researchers found that "only 17 percent of California workers who prevailed in their wage claims before the DLSE [California Division of Labor Standards Enforcement] and received a judgment were able to recover any payment at all between 2008 and 2011."[11]

So like so many Los Angeles workers, Billy and his coworkers let it go. Soon Billy too said goodbye to his boss and walked away from the job site. He'd lost a month's wages.

The week after he left, he started working for a different subcontractor of the same parent company. Just in time for our wedding.

* * *

Billy stood on the stage, fidgeting with a webcam. He'd hoped to live-stream our wedding to his parents and family in Guatemala, who had gathered together to celebrate in spirit, if not in person. But our technological capabilities fell short of our live-streaming dreams, and we couldn't get it to work. Instead, Billy and I pressed our heads together over a cell phone during our reception to hear his parents' words of joy and blessing.

Billy and I with our wedding party.

We thanked them and promised to deliver a DVD and attend a reception once we were able to visit Guatemala together.

Sadness and celebration. Pain and beauty. Heartache and joy. To be honest, I am grateful that these intermingle. Because sometimes the burdens facing our families, our neighbors, and our world feel crushing. As one who grew up isolated from so much of the world's pain, I often found myself overwhelmed when I encountered another tragedy or injustice. When I sat in an Atlanta public school room tutoring three illiterate sixth graders. When I heard stories of refugees who'd suffered loss of home, family separation, and violence. When I stood at the U.S.-Mexico border in Tijuana and looked at the endless crosses adorning the wall with the names of those missing or lost after they headed north to the United States. When my fiancé was denied pay he had earned and we saw no avenues for justice.

When the deep, heart-twisting realities of injustice, racism, and poverty settle in, it can feel as if you're suffocating. But there is nothing new under the sun. And while I may have felt righteous anger in the middle of the women's dress department, I am reminded that many resilient people have walked faithfully in the midst of suffering and persecution and injustice for generations. And they have much to teach us.

At one time or another, most of us have likely credited those living in hard circumstances for teaching us about contentment. Our service project and mission trip debriefings often include variations on the theme of how we should push away our disgruntled or disappointed thoughts because (thank God!) we don't have it as bad as the people we just served.

Yet while contentment is certainly an important lesson, I am convinced that people living on the margins have so much more to teach us than shallow gratefulness for material things. They can teach us how to hope. They can teach us how to anticipate justice while maintaining our dignity in the waiting. They can teach us how to fight. And they teach us how to celebrate and truly live amid unspeakable suffering.[12]

It is this steadfast resilience and belief in God's faithfulness that inspires me and that enriches the body of Christ. When our churches are too often divided by society's barriers, we miss so much from each other. Sometimes those who have experienced the most tragedy are the only ones who can truly teach us how to worship the Lord with delight. When we are isolated from groups who have deeply known suffering, can we truly know heart-drenching joy? We are incomplete in the body of Christ if we remain in our siloed communities defined by race, culture, country of origin, language, and socioeconomic status.

Once, at a party with Billy and his coworkers, I was amazed to watch these men whom I knew had experienced grueling conditions, mistreatment, and pay injustices celebrate together. They ate cake and sang songs while one guy strummed on the guitar. I was in awe of their resilience. No, I cannot look at neighbors and friends, some of whom struggle to make ends meet or face other withering challenges, and simply be grateful for the ways ease and comfort have permeated most of my life. No, I am taught how to party, how to lean in to community, how to continue to hope for God's goodness and grace when the headlines of the day suggest all good things are coming to an end.

The Sermon on the Mount reminds us what true blessings really are. *The Message* version says it like this:

> You're blessed when you're at the end of your rope. With less of you there is more of God and his rule.
>
> You're blessed when you feel you've lost what is most dear to you. Only then can you be embraced by the One most dear to you.

You're blessed when you're content with just who you are—no more, no less. That's the moment you find yourselves proud owners of everything that can't be bought.

You're blessed when you've worked up a good appetite for God. He's food and drink in the best meal you'll ever eat.

You're blessed when you care. At the moment of being "care-full," you find yourselves cared for.

You're blessed when you get your inside world—your mind and heart—put right. Then you can see God in the outside world.

You're blessed when you can show people how to cooperate instead of compete or fight. That's when you discover who you really are, and your place in God's family. (Matthew 5:3-9)

There is a place and a time to mourn injustice. Absolutely. There is a time to fight back against those who abuse and exploit the vulnerable. Of course. But that space cannot be the end of the journey.

We grieved the absence of family and loved ones who were not permitted to celebrate our wedding with us. And we strategized solutions for a corrupt system denying its workers the fruit of their labor. In the midst of these challenges, we were pushed to pray and hope and fight, all the while still celebrating with dignity and delight. Those who have suffered can teach us what it truly means to be blessed. They can teach us how to hope.

10

ALIEN RELATIVE

*A*fter the wedding, Billy and I returned to visit our lawyer, Mateo. He handed us a form: "Applying for an Alien Relative."

I stifled a giggle. I thought of my college friend Damaris, who had come to the States from Nicaragua when she was a toddler. She was an all-American girl whose rapid-fire Spanglish had blown my mind. Hers was the first immigrant church I ever attended, and she'd introduced me to a different American experience simply because we were friends. One day, she had looked at me earnestly. "Sarah, can I ask a question?"

I shrugged. "Of course."

"Why, in English, are we called 'aliens'?" I laughed. I had honestly never thought about it. I knew immigrants were sometimes referred to as aliens, but I'd never looked someone in the eye who was asking why they were described this way. Her serious expression made me regret laughing. Damaris continued, "It makes me think people think we're like weird freaks who aren't even from this planet."

I didn't have a good response. Of course I understood the formal use of the word, meaning "from a foreign land." But certainly, for most of us, a green science-fiction Martian is a more familiar association with the word *alien*. I saw the honest confusion in her face, and I hated to see how this word, linguistically correct though it may have been, contributed to a feeling of not belonging for someone who considered this her country.

When Billy read the form title, he smiled and rolled his eyes. He was then assigned an Alien number, more commonly called an A#, and we began climbing the mountain of paperwork that would have a significant impact on our future. We knew this course was likely to be straightforward, but there was still a nagging worry that initiating the official process made us vulnerable to the unknown, particularly the geographical location on which we'd build our life together.

"I need your addresses for the last five years," Mateo told us. We both began our lists: my apartment with friends, the room Billy had rented from a friend's mother, my school address, the house Billy had shared with his brother, the retirement home I'd lived in for a year, the pastor's address where Billy had first stayed in the States. We struggled to remember exact zip codes and match them with the correct street addresses. With a look of both amusement and concern, Mateo stopped us both at five each.

I had to submit my personal tax returns from the last couple of years and awkwardly ask my boss to write a letter to the government on my behalf, confirming my salary and that he wasn't planning to fire me anytime soon. I was surprised how much the application process seemed to focus on me rather than Billy. Mateo explained that I was actually the party submitting the petition and serving as a "sponsor" for my "alien relative." All the paperwork we were collecting was evidence to build a case that I was a suitable sponsor and that, as such, Billy would have no need to draw on any U.S. government assistance programs. I was again reminded that the road would be more difficult if we were struggling economically.

* * *

The Statue of Liberty is inscribed with these familiar words: "Give me your tired, your poor, your huddled masses yearning to breathe free, the wretched refuse of your teeming shore. Send these, the homeless, tempest-tossed to me, I lift my lamp beside the golden door!" This sentiment of welcome may resound with warmth and inspiration, but the immigration system itself works in direct opposition to this notion.

Lady Liberty was a gift from France to celebrate American democracy after the U.S. Civil War. However, it took about a decade to raise the funds for its creation and another ten years before the statue was completed by sculptor Frédéric-Auguste Bartholdi in 1885. In the meantime, U.S. citizens raised money to build the statue's pedestal. During a fundraising contest, Emma Lazarus submitted her 1883 poem "The New Colossus," a portion of which would become the famous inscription on the statue.[1]

Though the Statue of Liberty was becoming a beacon of welcome for those arriving at nearby Ellis Island, major shifts toward restricting immigration were already under way. The Chinese Exclusion Act was passed in 1882, suspending Chinese immigration for a decade.[2] Soon after, Congress passed the Immigration Act of 1882. This legislation "blocked (or excluded) the entry of idiots, lunatics, convicts, and persons likely to become a public charge."[3] Immigration enforcement had transitioned from individual states to the federal government, and new laws were including language to define which immigrants were "desirable" and who should be restricted from entering the country.

But it's the phrase "persons likely to become a public charge" that shaped the immigration system in such a way as to actively deny poor immigrants. Those entering the United States needed to be able to prove they could support themselves (or had someone to support them) and would in no way require support from the government. As Billy and I completed the forms for an alien relative, it was clear that "Give me your tired, your poor, your huddled masses" was really "Give me your self-sufficient, your financially independent, your innovative entrepreneurs."

* * *

Billy, we were told, would receive notifications in the mail to show up for fingerprinting appointments, as well as a medical physical. "We have insurance," Billy told the lawyer. "Can I go to my doctor for a physical?"

"No," Mateo said. "You may not use your own doctor. There are specific immigration doctors that you must see. You will need to pay them directly when you go to your appointment."

We sighed. We had tried to be ultraresponsible with the wedding gifts we'd received, saving checks to cover the expense of our immigration process. One gift had included a note, "Buy something that will last a long time!" We laughed as we added it to our "green card fund." But the costs were quickly adding up, and our wedding money was dwindling with every visit to the lawyer's office. Replace the missing I-94: $445. Petition for an alien relative: $535. Apply for permanent residence: $1,140. Fingerprinting: $85. More forms. Lawyer's fees. Doctor's appointments. In total, we paid close to $3,000 for the process.[4]

Mateo asked us to stand against the wall and pose for individual photos without smiling. Naturally, the "no teeth" requirement sent me into fits of uncontrolled laughter. Mateo smiled patiently, but my giggles betrayed my nerves and my sense of how ridiculous this experience was becoming. Never had I expected my nuptials to require so many forms, physicals, fingerprints, and mug shots. This early hurdle in our marriage experience was unfamiliar to me, and to pretty much everyone I'd known, in every way.

I squelched my laughter and took a smileless photo.

* * *

While I may not have known anyone who had gone through this process, it's estimated that more than 16 million people live in mixed-status families—families with at least one unauthorized immigrant.[5] Billy and I were considered a mixed-status couple, but we are only one iteration of mixed-status families. Many U.S. citizen children are living in the country with undocumented parents. In her moving memoir, *In the Country We Love*, actor Diane Guerrero shares her harrowing personal story of returning home from school one day when she was fourteen years old to discover a surprisingly empty house. Both of her parents had been arrested during the day, a neighbor informed her. Even though she was a U.S. citizen and a minor, no one from Immigration or Child Protective Services came to check on her. Instead, she hid under her bed with a cordless phone until her friend's mother arrived.[6]

Outdated immigration laws do not address mixed-status families like Guerrero's. After the proposed Immigration Act of 2007 died in Congress, subsequent efforts to pass immigration reform similarly failed, leaving the country with antiquated immigration laws that haven't been comprehensively updated since 1996—for context, since before Facebook and YouTube existed. In response to congressional inaction, President Barack Obama initiated an executive order in 2014 to provide temporary relief for undocumented parents of U.S. citizen children. This order was called Deferred Action for Parents of Americans and Lawful Permanent Residents, or DAPA. DAPA sought to protect nuclear families by preventing parents from being removed from their children. Between 2003 and 2013, estimates suggest that somewhere between 750,000 to 925,000 parents—typically fathers—of U.S. citizens were deported.[7] These forced family separations have a significant impact on children in every way, including financial insecurity, emotional upheaval, and even physical relocation, as many kids move in with distant relatives or are enrolled in the foster care system.

DAPA was frozen in February 2015 after Texas and twenty-five other states banded together to challenge the president's order. Parents of U.S. citizens remained vulnerable to deportation while the DAPA challenge traveled to the Supreme Court, which heard arguments in April 2016 to decide whether the executive order was constitutional. If upheld, approximately 3.7 million immigrant parents would have had the opportunity to apply for temporary work authorization through DAPA.[8] However, the Supreme Court deadlocked in a 4–4 tie on June 23, 2016, sending the case back to the lower courts.[9] As a final nail in the coffin, DAPA was officially rescinded on June 15, 2017, in a memorandum from the secretary of Homeland Security.[10] The program was never enacted.

* * *

Why should Christians pay attention to these legislative battles? Because, as it turns out, the American church is also a mixed-status family.

The American church community—our church family—includes generational U.S. citizens, undocumented immigrants, naturalized U.S. citizens, legal permanent residents, mixed-status couples, and U.S. citizen children with undocumented parents. According to the Pew Research Center, undocumented immigrants "come primarily from Latin America and the Caribbean, and the overwhelming majority of them, an estimated 83 percent, are Christian."[11] Many of the immigrant families in our midst find support and encouragement in their faith, especially during crisis.

It doesn't matter whether we understand or support every family's situation or whether we agree on how reform should be legislated. We are first and foremost a family. Our call as Christians to care for our brothers and sisters does not hold conditions, nor does it change with the political climate. In 1 John 4:19-21, the apostle reminds us, "We love because he first loved us. If anyone says, 'I love God,' and hates his brother, he is a liar; for he who does not love his brother whom he has seen cannot love God whom he has not seen. And this commandment we have from him: whoever loves God must also love his brother."

When we acknowledge the struggles in our extended family, we share the burden and carry the stress of knowing that others in our own church family are at risk. We have stories in the Bible of families who were in danger of being separated forever because of political leaders' fears. In Exodus, the Egyptian pharaoh grew nervous about Israelites in his land. He declared their growing numbers were a threat, and announced, "Come, let us deal shrewdly with them" (Exodus 1:10). He then decreed that all Hebrew infant boys be killed.

Jochebed, a Hebrew mother of a young girl named Miriam and a little boy named Aaron, had recently given birth to another son. With this imminent danger hanging over Moses's infant head, Jochebed did what any mother would do: she hid her baby and tried to get him to safety. No one else in Moses's family was marked for death. Still, they participated fully in his rescue because they were a family. Moses's parents hid him from authorities for three months. And it was Moses's sister, Miriam, who stood by and protected her baby brother from the threat of harm. What strikes me is when we see Moses's parents mentioned later in Hebrews 11, which is often referred to as "the faith chapter." The writer of Hebrews praises this family's bravery and tells us they acted in the way they did because they had faith and were not afraid of the king's edict (11:23).

As we hear the stories of our brothers and sisters fleeing to the United States to escape military extremists, gang violence, or famine and starvation, we experience this suffering as a family. Those who have violated immigration laws to save their lives or the lives of their children make us, the church, a mixed-status family. This solidarity, birthed in the kinship of the kingdom, makes it impossible to ignore the crushing edicts that harm our family. When we said yes to Jesus, we signed the form acknowledging our alien relatives.

And the Scriptures encourage us, "Keep on loving each other as brothers and sisters. Don't forget to show hospitality to strangers, for some who have done this have entertained angels without realizing it! Remember those in prison, as if you were there yourself. Remember also those being mistreated, as if you felt their pain in your own bodies" (Hebrews 13:1-3 NLT). This invitation to solidarity with our family is a foundational tenet of the church.

* * *

As Billy and I prepared for our immigration interview, we spoke with other couples who had gone through the process. We were advised to make sure we were on the same page about how we met, the names of those in our wedding party, and where we visited on our honeymoon. Veterans also encouraged us to study our house and to be ready for questions about where we kept the salt and on which side of the bed our partner slept.

We were warned the interviewer might try to rattle us or throw us off our game. "What color panties is your wife wearing today?" was a question one husband was asked. Another friend shared how the agent tried to rile him by insinuating that perhaps his wife had been working as a prostitute, since they had waited seven years after getting married to apply for her green card. So we steeled ourselves for anything we thought they might try to use against us.

We knew it was the government official's job to ask the mundane and intimate questions in order to determine whether our love was true or an immigration scam. Still, we felt vulnerable at the idea of a government employee leading us through an official and high-stakes version of *The Newlywed Game*. We had nothing to hide, but we couldn't quell the anxiety. So much was riding on this one-shot interview. We couldn't afford to be sloppy. One mistake could have severe and far-reaching consequences.

* * *

We walked into a large white room lit with a fluorescent glare. I glanced around at all the mixed-status couples occupying the rows of folding chairs. Most people stared at the news program on the TV, while others read or rested their eyes. All of us held stacks of bills, photo albums, and other evidence of our true love. I gripped the endless pages our lawyer had prepared and completed for this meeting. I'd spent an hour at a print shop the week before, selecting photos from my thumb drive: our date to Catalina Island, our wedding, my sister's wedding with Billy in the family photos, camping trips with friends. The images were carefully organized inside a lime-green photo album. I knew it was nothing that someone with Photoshop and a good printer couldn't fabricate. But I had to hope it would be enough.

After an hour, I whispered to Billy that I wanted to ask other couples to see their wedding albums. Too tense and nervous to be amused, he looked at me like I was crazy. But I studied the couple speaking both a European language and English to their children, a white man cuddling with an Asian woman, and another couple who appeared, like us, to be a Latino man and a white woman. Everyone had their photo albums easily accessible, and I wanted to know all their stories. But everyone was awaiting their moment in front of an official, so we sat quietly next to our spouses.

As our wait time grew, Billy and I concocted theories about why we were having to wait so long. "Do you think they have cameras in the room to watch us?" Billy whispered. Convinced the interview had already begun, he put his arm around me. Then he put it down, worried it would look like we were trying too hard. How did a real husband act? Billy had no idea, and we were unraveling under the pressure. Mercifully, they called our number, and we walked back to meet our interviewer.

The agent barely looked up as she reached out for our folder. "Sorry for the wait," she said. "A couple folks left early today, and we're very busy." I exhaled, glad to know no one was evaluating our footage to question us about our awkward waiting room behavior.

"Name?" She nodded toward Billy. He listed all four of his names.

"Birth date?"

Billy started to answer by listing a few months and days and backtracking to say different months, different days. I looked over at him with wide, panicked eyes. He was so nervous that he was confusing his own birthday, mine, our wedding date, and other random numbers. He stopped. "I'm sorry," he said, and let out a small laugh. "I'm just really nervous."

She looked up and offered a curt smile. "So when's your birthday?"

He answered correctly. He looked at me and raised his eyebrows. She flipped through the scores of pages in our file. I squeezed our album on my lap. She asked a clarifying question. We answered. She licked her thumb, plucked out a couple of the papers from the stack, and left the room.

Billy and I glanced at each other but waited in heavy silence. There may not have been cameras in the waiting room, but we weren't taking any chances in the office. She whisked back into room but didn't sit down. We stood up. "Here are your originals back," she said, handing Billy the pieces of paper she'd taken. "I made copies." She held up another sheet. "This piece of paper will serve as your temporary residence card until the real one arrives in the mail. I will need to take your work permit. You won't need it now."

I almost gasped. We had hardly been asked any questions! I had been ready to wow her with all the random facts I'd memorized about my beloved, but now our interview seemed to be winding down. I was almost disappointed, and I was tempted to push my photo album into her hands just to show off my mad scrapbooking skills. But I resisted and stayed quiet.

Billy hesitated before reluctantly turning over his work permit, which had only been recently issued to allow him legalized presence in the country while we went through the immigration process. We accepted a printed piece of paper and a promise in its place.

11

HIDING IN PLAIN SIGHT

*Y*olanda, an undocumented mother from Guatemala, led us through the church. My students walked quietly behind her, squeezing through the doorframes to a less public part of the building. There, behind the choir loft, Yolanda allowed us a glimpse of the room where she and her seventeen-year-old daughter were living. Then she sat down in a folding chair, my students forming a semicircle around her in their own chairs, and told us her story.

When Yolanda received her deportation orders, she feared being separated from her daughter, who is a U.S. citizen. She was evaluating her options for avoiding deportation when her church, Immanuel Presbyterian in Los Angeles, offered to let her live in their building. Churches are considered "sensitive locations." A memorandum from U.S. Immigration and Customs Enforcement (also known as ICE) seeks to ensure that "enforcement actions do not occur at nor are focused on sensitive locations such as schools and churches," with a few exceptions.[1] This policy gives some limited protections for people like Yolanda, who are living in churches as part of the New Sanctuary Movement. Yolanda gave up her freedom, essentially living under house arrest for years while she tried to adjust her legal situation, be present for her daughter, and advocate for other immigrants in her similar situation.

Alexia Salvatierra is a cofounder of the New Sanctuary Movement, an interfaith effort that now includes eight hundred congregations, in thirty cities, that are committed to protecting and standing with undocumented immigrants. In an interview, Salvatierra explained that "the concept of sanctuary comes from Numbers, which is a prescription for the people of God to act when someone has committed a crime, but the response to that crime is cruel and unusual punishment. In Numbers, the crime committed was manslaughter. People who had killed someone accidentally were being punished as if they had killed intentionally."[2]

In the text, God instructs Moses and the Israelites to give the Levites towns and pasturelands on which they can live (Numbers 35:2-5). Then God says, "You shall select cities to be cities of refuge for you, that the manslayer who kills any person without intent may flee there. The cities shall be for you a refuge from the avenger, that the manslayer may not die until he stands before the congregation for judgment" (Numbers 35:11-12). At that time, tribal law dictated that if someone was killed, that person's death must be avenged by someone from the tribe.[3] This categorical rendering of the law did not allow for any nuance when the crime committed was actually manslaughter. So God instructed the Israelites to protect people whose circumstances were clear-cut according to tribal law but whose backstory was a little more complicated and who deserved to have their case heard. "This passage," said Salvatierra, "is the basis for sanctuary work, protecting those who have committed a crime, but where the punishment is cruel and unusual."[4]

Yolanda was part of the second wave of the movement, also called the New Sanctuary Movement. The original Sanctuary Movement was born in the 1980s, when the civil wars in Central America pushed migrants to flee to safety in the United States. In the wake of mass killings in their home countries, people left their homes to seek security elsewhere. Judith McDaniel, author of *Sanctuary: A Journey*, writes about the initial incident that prompted the movement. A group of Salvadoran immigrants had been abandoned by their guide in the treacherous desert terrain of Organ Pipe Cactus National Monument in Arizona.[5] Thirteen people—nine women and four men—died after being left without food, water, or directions to safety. Temperatures were reported to have been 110 degrees or higher while the migrants searched for shade and water in the remote region. Thirteen other travelers survived, and eventually one woman came to a state highway and was able to flag down a driver, who alerted Border Patrol.

This tragedy made headlines in the United States, and many churches immediately sought to help the Salvadorans who had survived. But advocates soon learned that the migrants were about to be deported back to El Salvador without even the opportunity to apply for asylum status. According to McDaniel, "The churches thought these refugees should have been protected under the 1980 Refugee Act and other applicable laws, which provide asylum for any refugee who can demonstrate a 'well-founded fear of persecution.'"[6] Local Arizona congregations began to collaborate to assist immigrants and refugees. Then, on March 24, 1982, six churches adopted the title of "sanctuaries" to build communities of refuge and support for immigrants fleeing persecution and violence.[7] This gutsy act of hospitality and care ignited the Sanctuary Movement.

* * *

I have watched the courage and bravery of pastors and lay leaders who have stood at the forefront of the New Sanctuary Movement, both when I first met Yolanda back in 2007 and more recently as a third wave of the movement gained momentum in 2017.

I have admired the conviction of Christians in the New Sanctuary Movement that what they are doing is right . . . while silently wondering if it is. Isn't it too risky? Is this really the right way to do things? In all honesty, I have at times struggled with understanding and engaging the movement. It's one thing to treat immigrants with love and kindness regardless of their legal status. Isn't it something entirely different to protect them from the legal ramifications of their situation? It's one thing to extend mercy and love to those on the margins. Isn't it something entirely different for Christians to knowingly sidestep the law of the land?

But when I sit with these thoughts, I cannot avoid the nagging feeling that my worry is less about the question "Should I protect others?" and more about "Will I be protected?" During the first wave of the Sanctuary Movement in the 1980s, sixteen people, including clergy and laypersons, were eventually indicted on charges, including conspiracy. None served any prison time, but eight were convicted.[8] I worry about the ways that, if I stand up for someone else, I might suffer consequences in my own life.

When I first sat in our lawyer's office and learned we might have to move to Guatemala as a repercussion of Billy's status, I was blindsided. It wasn't how I'd imagined my first decade of marriage. But I felt at peace that we would be doing the right thing, pursuing legal status through the proper channels, even if that meant we were forced to accept exile status for a time. On the other hand, when Billy's boss asked me to share my Social

Security number, I felt a similar assurance that breaking the law in that case was not the right path for us. We would maintain our integrity and trust God to work out the details.

But where are those lines between doing the right thing, addressing injustices, risking one's own security, protecting the vulnerable, and breaking the law? If I had lived in the tribal culture referenced in the book of Numbers, how would I have acted if someone was to be murdered in retribution for accidentally killing someone? Would I have risked my own safety and followed God's countercultural sanctuary from the brutal execution of the law? Or would I have stood off to the side, saying "What a pity" and feeling that my hands were tied? Because, well, after all, it was the law of the land.

* * *

I have always admired Queen Esther. In my early days of attending fall festivals at church, she was my go-to Bible character to dress up as. In fact, so deep was my commitment to recreating my vision of her queenly appearance that I felt a passionate need to address my lack of pierced ears. I rolled aluminum foil into stunning spheres and pierced them with paper clips, which I then clipped on my ears. My throbbing, red lobes were the first example of the personal sacrifice I was willing to endure to emulate Queen Esther.

As an adult, though, I read her story with a new perspective (and legitimately pierced ears) and was taken aback. This woman of God I had so admired was much more than a girl who won a beauty pageant.

Indeed, Esther's story essentially starts with an ancient version of Miss Persia. The king's men suggest that local virgins be brought to the king, and Esther is among the initial group of contestants. Then she's on to round two. "And the young woman pleased him and won his favor. And he quickly provided her with her cosmetics and her portion of food, and with seven chosen young women from the king's palace, and advanced her and her young women to the best place in the harem" (Esther 2:9).

Then the women spend one year undergoing beauty treatments before their overnight date with the king. Esther goes to see the king, and he is blown away by her. The Scriptures say he loved her "more than all the other women" and that she "won grace and favor in his sight." With that declaration, it is no surprise when she is declared the winner. The king "set the royal crown on her head and made her queen" (Esther 2:17).

Life is going pretty well for Esther. Everyone really likes her (Esther 2:15). She's got a husband who loves her more than he loves other women—which is a pretty big deal in those days, since he's the king and all. And she's been elevated to a position of prestige and honor. Things are also going pretty well for her cousin Mordecai, who raised her like a daughter. He has uncovered a plot to kill the king and passed it along to Esther. She notifies the authorities, and when the rumors are found to be true, the conspirators are hanged and Mordecai's faithfulness is recorded (Esther 2:21-23).

Esther and Mordecai are Jews, but Esther has hidden this identity from the king on Mordecai's instruction. However, Mordecai's business is about to be laid bare. The king had commanded that people bow down to Haman, one of the king's men. But Mordecai defies this decree. "Then the king's servants who were at the king's gate said to Mordecai, 'Why do you transgress the king's command?'" (Esther 3:3).

For most modern-day Christians, it is not hard to understand this type of civil disobedience. We have witnessed biblical figures like Daniel and Shadrach, Meshach, and Abednego defy public orders to worship political leaders in place of God. This type of lawbreaking seems pretty cut and dried. And the Bible stories in which Daniel survives a night in the pit with lions and the three young men are accompanied by an angel in the fiery furnace—these seem to confirm the idea that God protects those who break the law to honor God.

Mordecai, however, is not punished on a personal level. In fact, Esther 3:6 says, "But he [Haman] disdained to lay hands on Mordecai alone. So, as they had made known to him the people of Mordecai, Haman sought to destroy all the Jews, the people of Mordecai, throughout the whole kingdom of Ahasuerus."

What happens next speaks to what we see happening with foreign residents today. Haman approaches King Ahasuerus and lays out the threat: "There is a certain people scattered abroad and dispersed among the peoples in all the provinces of your kingdom. Their laws are different from those of every other people, and they do not keep the king's laws, so that it is not to the king's profit to tolerate them. If it please the king, let it be decreed that they be destroyed" (Esther 3:8-9). The king responds by essentially telling Haman, "Do what you need to do," and he hands him the authority to make laws on behalf of the king with his signet ring. "Letters were sent by couriers to all the king's provinces with instruction to destroy, to kill, and to annihilate all Jews, young and old, women and children, in one day" (Esther 3:13).

A president's rhetoric about deporting "almost everyone" has led to executive orders that open the door to this type of indiscriminate deportation. These words and actions have been experienced by many immigrants in a way similar to the way that Jews experienced Haman's edict. This comparison may sound like an exaggeration; after all, deportation is not the same thing as annihilation. But for many people, returning to places like El Salvador and Guatemala, which continue to struggle with violence, deportation orders read like nothing less than death sentences.

El Refugio ("The Refuge") is a ministry that coordinates volunteers to visit detainees in immigration detention. It also provides hospitality to families in need of a meal or place to stay while visiting loved ones at the detention center.[9] In a 2017 article for Religion News Service, El Refugio board chair Marie Marquardt describes Moises, a young man from El Salvador with whom volunteers in the organization had built a relationship. Moises had fled to the States after gang members who were extorting his mother, a local food vendor, began to harass him and threaten his life. He sought refuge in the States and petitioned for asylum status. Despite assistance from El Refugio and evidence of his credible fear, his asylum claim was denied and he was deported.

Back in El Salvador, Moises essentially lived as a recluse, hiding in his family's home for almost three years. Then, on November 26, 2016, he decided to go to dinner with his best friend. They were abducted by gang members. Marquardt writes,

> In the final weeks of 2016, while we frantically prepared to celebrate the holidays, our friend Moises was found murdered on a neighborhood street in San Salvador. Twenty-two bullet holes perforated his young body. When his older brother called from El Salvador to share the devastating news, he made one request.
>
> "Tell the judge [Moises] wasn't lying. Tell the judge he told the truth."[10]

* * *

President Trump's 2017 "Border Security and Immigration Enforcement Improvements" executive order removed some of the administrative options that allowed for discretion and nuance in the immigration legal system. Without these simple protections, the focus on mass deportation rings very similar to Haman's edict to "destroy, kill, and annihilate." It's no surprise, then, that immigration advocates have been mourning loudly. In the same way, "Mordecai tore his clothes and put on sackcloth and ashes, and went out into the midst of the city, and he cried out with a loud and bitter cry" (Esther 4:1).

It is in this context that the third wave of the Sanctuary Movement has blossomed. When we spoke, Alexia Salvatierra noted the passion and compassion sweeping through people of faith. "Churches really want to help and have been asking, 'What can we do? How can we provide legal help, discourage the worst abuses, bring light to the stories of what's happening?'"[11] She noted that some churches have been going behind the scenes to obtain power of attorney so that children don't enter the foster care system if their parents are deported. Some pastors are making their presence known near local schools so they can comfort families, as well as serve as a discouragement to immigration officials who might target families whose children are trying to attend school. In addition, as Yolanda and others had done, new families have taken up residence in churches.

Salvatierra defines two types of sanctuary. Some individuals or families enter into "private sanctuary," where they may move quietly into a church in order to take a temporary break. "It's an opportunity to try to find legal help or to give them a reprieve as they figure out next steps," she said. The other example is that of those, like Yolanda, who live in "public sanctuary." They consent to sharing their stories while living inside the church and seeking assistance with their legal situation. The attention on their experiences, along with the example of nonimmigrants standing with someone in sanctuary, often encourages other citizens to take a second look at the issue.

When I asked Salvatierra about those who consider the New Sanctuary Movement an example of harboring criminals, she explained, "Harboring is concealing someone with the purpose of furthering their illegal presence in this country. First of all, in public sanctuary, we don't conceal people. It is not illegal for the church to offer humanitarian services or to allow someone to sleep inside their building. And secondly, we're not attempting to further their illegal presence in this country because we're working to legalize their status. We're both trying to change the laws and working with them individually to see if there's a way for them to stay legally."

For many Christians, the answer still might not seem quite so simple. Is it right to help someone who entered the country illegally hide from law enforcement, even if you're working with lawyers to try to help the person resolve things legally? Somehow these situations may not feel as clear as supporting people of faith who refuse to bow down to other gods.

But I am drawn back to Esther. Mordecai sends word to Esther about how the Jews are on the verge of destruction. He tells her the details and even presents a copy of the written decree that details how their very lives are at risk. And then he begs her to go to the king and beseech him on behalf of the Jews (Esther 4:6-8).

Her response? It is against the law! Esther reminds Mordecai that if she approaches the king without being summoned, the law would support her being put to death unless the king chooses to show her mercy (Esther 4:10-11). It's too risky. It's not the right way to do things. She doesn't offer another solution, but it's clear she's afraid for her own life.

I can relate. I worry what might happen to me if I get "too carried away" in advocating for justice for the Other. I want to follow the letter of the law, even when I'm presented with the evidence of real suffering around me. Situations seem overwhelming when considered from the magnitude of a national movement or social justice cause. However, when we are connected to those on the margins through real relationships, the idea of standing between our friends and death doesn't raise the same types of questions or hesitations.

A popular quote from Mother Teresa says, "If we have no peace, it is because we have forgotten that we belong to each other." It is easier to turn away from the hurting when I feel I have no tie to their situation. Sometimes we need to be reminded of our connectedness to those who are suffering. Mordecai has to tell Esther the same thing. "Do not think to yourself that in the king's palace you will escape any more than all the other Jews. For if you keep silent at this time, relief and deliverance will rise for the Jews from another place, but you and your father's house will perish. And who knows whether you have not come to the kingdom for such a time as this?" (Esther 4:13-14). In this powerful speech, Mordecai points out Esther's position of privilege while reminding her that she is related to those who are in danger.

It is then that I imagine Esther rising up and holding her scepter, her face raised to the sky. She accepts the call to put herself between power and the vulnerable. She has made her decision. "I will go to the king, though it is against the law, and if I perish, I perish" (Esther 4:16).

Oh, that I could have the courage of Esther. Christ continues to ask me to die to myself, to put my own safety and comfort on the back burner so that I might join the story God is writing. I am inspired by the example of this woman, who could have so easily returned to her perfumed baths and tried to ignore the cries of those around her. But, instead, she identified more deeply with people on the margins than with the comforts to which she had become accustomed.

Some might have criticized her for breaking the law and approaching the king. It wasn't the proper way, the right thing to do. Some people of faith have sharply denounced the New Sanctuary Movement and the ways that other Christians are seeking to come alongside undocumented immigrants. But as we seek to follow a selfless Christ, who laid down his life for others, we must consider his call to compassion in the face of deportation orders, family separations, and divisions between neighbors.

12

FENCES AND WALLS

*Y*ou've got mail!" I practically screamed into the phone one Friday afternoon. I was like an overcaffeinated Meg Ryan. Billy was slow to ramp up to my level of enthusiasm. I could hear him shuffling and moving away from the loud construction equipment in the background.

"What?" he asked when he got a distance away and it was a bit quieter.

"You got a letter from Immigration," I told him.

"What is it?"

"I don't know. I didn't open it."

"What?"

"Well, I don't know," I said. "It's a federal crime to open someone else's mail."

"Sarah," he said before bursting into laughter. "Open it!"

When I started to rip open the envelope, I realized my hands were shaking. Carefully, I pulled out the letter and his newly minted green card. There I stood, in the middle of our tiny L.A. dining room, just staring at it. For a moment I was quiet.

"It's here," I said so softly it was almost a whisper. And I started crying. "It's here."

The card itself wasn't particularly noteworthy. It wasn't even green. But I felt as if I held the whole world in my hands. I exhaled a fragile breath. I could finally lay to rest all the silent but ever-present thoughts that had plagued me: What if he gets deported? What would my life in Guatemala look like? Will this process ever end? I felt an unexpected lightness.

"Woo hoo!" Billy shouted over the phone, awakening me from my reverie. "Let's go to Mexico!" Naturally. There I was, a young wife basking in the relief that my husband could finally get a driver's license for all that massive construction equipment he drove around Southern California. I was feeling peace that we were headed toward safety and away from the uncertainty and risk that had characterized our first months together. But his first thought was, Let's test it out! "I get off work at seven," he continued. "I'll head home, and we can drive to San Diego. We'll go to Mexico in the morning!"

I held the phone between my ear and shoulder and turned the card over in my hands. The U.S. government had processed all our paperwork, cashed all our checks, and listened to all our interview responses. They had decided we were not a fraud. We were free. Free to go to Mexico on a whim. "I'm in!" I told Billy.

The next morning, we were chatting and driving when we observed roadside signs in Spanish and realized we must have crossed the border. It was almost painful to realize how simple it was to enter Mexico. We hadn't had to talk with an officer. We weren't held in detention until our case could be evaluated. We hadn't even had to pump the brakes.[1]

Billy navigated the streets of Tijuana as we explored our newfound freedom. We sat on stools at an outdoor dining establishment in which the servers were clearly accustomed to more of a spring break sort of crowd. Even though it was eleven in the morning on a random Saturday and we were the sole customers, our waiter worked hard to hype us up with over-the-top jokes and suggestive drinking games. I learned how wonderful it could be to travel with someone who knew more Spanish than "¿Dónde está la playa?" (Where is the beach?) when Billy said in Spanish, "Thanks, man, for *all this*, but could we maybe get some Cokes . . . and more salsa?"

* * *

We did actually find *la playa*, and we checked out beachfront condos, dreaming of a retirement within view of the ocean. As we continued driving along the shoreline, we accidentally stumbled upon the westernmost point of the U.S.-Mexico border.

I had been there before, with a group of students during a course focused on immigration. While my students and I were visiting this area where the border fence cuts through the sand and jets out into the water, a young man had struck up a conversation with us. As it turned out, he was also from Los Angeles and was a former legal permanent resident of the United States who, as he described it, had "messed up" and then was deported. I didn't question his story because I knew it was possible for legal permanent residents to lose their status. The typical reason is that they have committed a crime.

He was a young guy, probably in his late twenties, and he had openly shared with our group how he was waiting there at the beach, planning to cross the border. "I have nothing in Mexico," he told us. "I came to the States as a small child, and I've lived my whole life there. My mom is there. My kid is there. I've been trying to cross every day since I got deported, and I will keep doing it every day until I get home."

The border is highly contested and politicized space. It is heavily symbolic, but it is also inescapably meaningful to real people. To committed officers working hard to do their job and protect the border. To young fathers sitting at the beach, trying to figure out how to get home. In the midst of real-life stories, however, there is intense rhetoric and political flair.

Promises of harsh border enforcement have long made compelling political messaging. But sometimes those efforts stray from the truth in order to make a point or connect with fearful voters. Most recently, Donald Trump made illegal immigration a pillar of his presidential campaign. In his first campaign ad, a deep-voiced narrator promises, "He'll stop illegal immigration by building a wall on our southern border that Mexico *will* pay for."[2] The visuals during the first part of the sentence show hordes of people sitting on top of a wall. At the words "our southern border," the video cuts to an aerial image of approximately fifty people running toward the border wall. The fact-checking website PolitiFact traced the footage back to its

My students and I visited the westernmost point of the U.S.-Mexico border.

original airing on an Italian television network. Writer Carolyn Edds notes, "The clear suggestion is that the footage is of the 'southern border' between the United States and Mexico. But it's not—it's 5,000 miles away, in a small Spanish enclave on the mainland of Morocco."[3] Border enforcement is a real need. But manipulative narratives only distort the situation and complicate the response. Often, the immediate goal is to secure outrageous amounts of federal funding for border enforcement. Unfortunately, many of the funded measures do little to address root issues or the actual ways undocumented immigrants are entering the country.

* * *

During the visit to Tijuana with my students, we stood at another section of the border, still on the Mexican side but in the middle of the city and away from the beach. In the distance, the secondary wall (yes, this area contains not one but two border fences) was cold and nondescript, with slanted fencing and coils of barbed wire on top. Tall watchtowers with stadium lights and video surveillance rose into the sky. Cameras, manned 24/7, kept a watchful eye on the flat land, along with roving Border Patrol agents in white SUVs.[4] Officials used night vision technology once the sun set.

Unlike the secondary wall, however, the primary fence was covered in art. On the Mexican side of the border, we were able to walk right up to this wall, which was made of corrugated metal. I was surprised by the vast difference between the two walls—and, in particular, with the art that traveled along the Mexican side. Large white crosses stretched down the fence, with names painted on each one. Each cross represented an individual life that had been lost while attempting to cross the border. Full-sized caskets attached to the fence commemorated the collective deaths annually, each one citing a year and its corresponding death toll.

In the years since my visit with my students, art has continued to bloom along the wall. Some pieces focus less on border-crossing deaths and more on the relationship between the United States and Mexico, as well as the impact of immigration on Mexicans. Murals call on the Mexican government to take responsibility for the lives lost with a focus on local job creation and public safety. Another political piece of artwork on the wall quotes the derogatory words Donald Trump used during his presidential campaign to describe Mexican immigrants. Other artwork on the wall is more inspirational, such as one optical illusion that makes the fencing disappear into a beautiful landscape.

One small image on the wall repurposes the iconic caution sign depicting a silhouette of an immigrant family crossing the border. It's a familiar image to many residents of Southern California. Leslie Berestein of the *San Diego Union-Tribune* describes it this way: "A ghostly silhouette of a mother, father and little girl running, their bodies leaning forward as if into the wind. The child's pigtails fly behind her as the family dashes across a stark yellow background, accompanied by one word: CAUTION."[5]

These signs were erected, especially along I-5 in California, in the 1990s when officials were hoping to reduce deaths at places where immigrants would sometimes dart into traffic to avoid border security. Smugglers, seeing an immigration checkpoint ahead, would sometimes slow the car and tell passengers to get out and run toward the beach to bypass the checkpoint before meeting up again on the other side. Many immigrants were unaccustomed to the speed and danger of U.S. freeways, and some didn't make it. In an attempt to stop these deaths, this now recognizable sign was created. But on the border fence, one Mexican artist depicts this same family holding on to a bundle of balloons and being lifted over the fence.[6]

The wall itself has been used as a symbolic element of immigration enforcement as much as, if not more than, a practical one. While on the campaign trail, Trump told the *New York Times*'s editorial board that he relied on the U.S.-Mexico border wall to revive waning crowds at his rallies. The *Times* quoted him: "'You know,' he said of his events, 'if it gets a little boring, if I see people starting to sort of, maybe thinking about leaving, I can sort of tell the audience, I just say, "We will build the wall!" and they go nuts.'"[7] The slogan "Build the wall!" was a key element of his campaign, and he represented the border as a porous and unguarded space.

In reality, in places like Tijuana where my students and I stood, I wonder if taxpayers will be funding the construction of a third wall. Or perhaps the new construction will only pick up in the places where rugged terrain has made it too challenging and unnecessary for building walls in the past. Of course, this focus on the border does not address illegal entries through other methods, such as underground tunnels, and, of course, overstayed visas.

But contrary to narratives that depict the U.S.-Mexico border as out of control, things have changed significantly over the last decade. According to the Migration Policy Institute, the United States spent nearly $187 billion on federal immigration enforcement between 1987 and 2013, more than it spent on all other federal criminal law enforcement agencies—including the FBI and DEA—combined.[8] These funds cover a range of enforcement needs, such as agents, ground sensors, surveillance equipment, drones, helicopters, and more.[9]

After digging into a Department of Homeland Security report, Daniel González of the *Arizona Republic* found that "the number of successful illegal entries—including people making multiple attempts—between ports of entry along the entire southern border with Mexico has plummeted from 1.7 million in 2005 to 170,000 in 2015."[10] He notes that this data does not include unaccompanied minors and families who turned themselves in at the border to seek asylum status.

* * *

I sat down at the long table with my paper plate in hand. Glancing around, I did a quick head count of my college students. After visiting the border, our group had come to a shelter that provided temporary lodging and hospitality to men who had been deported from the United States.

We had met earlier in the day with the priest who ran the facility. Most of the men sleeping and performing chores in the building's courtyard were essentially penniless, and many were very far from home. Though deposited just across the border in Tijuana, deportees were originally from all over the country. Men found a bed and a meal at this shelter while they considered their next move. There was cost and risk both with making plans to travel home and with attempting to return to the United States under the radar.

Now we were all sitting with strangers, breaking bread at this Tijuana table. I was uncomfortable. I knew the man sitting in front me either had been deported or had failed at crossing the border successfully. He knew I knew this part of his story, but he knew nothing about me. I made shy eye contact and dusted off my weak Spanish to try to start a conversation. We clumsily chatted about our families and our experiences in the

States. All around the dining room, folks scraped plates clean and quiet voices hummed as my students held similar conversations with the men.

Later, as we debriefed the visit, a small group of students shared that the man they were eating with had asked where they were from. When they told him the name of the Southern California city where our small college was located, his face fell and he dropped his head. "My wife and kids live there," he'd said in clear English. "And tonight you all will just drive back there."

Recounting this conversation to the group, my students let that statement hang in the air. Then one student spoke. "It was so awkward when he said that," she admitted. "It became so obvious how different things are because we were born in different places. And the fact that he can't see his family. . ." Her voice trailed off, but several others nodded in silence.

Sharing a meal with these men, we were equals, travelers together on this road of life. But this stark reality—our freedom to drive and to return home after a day on the other side of the border—was inescapable. Meanwhile, this man was left behind, separated from his loved ones and trying to gauge his next, dangerous move.

* * *

Billy and I sat on a concrete stoop, watching the Pacific waves lap at the tall pillars extending into the ocean to divide the United States and Mexico. Border Patrol trucks rumbled on the U.S. side of the fence while we watched people wander through Friendship Park, a designated binational meeting space at the border.[11]

First lady Pat Nixon dedicated this section of the border on the beach in 1971. "May there never be a wall between these two great nations," she said in that ceremony. "Only friendship."[12]

This section of the border is the only area where citizens on the U.S. side can approach the fence and where the slats are wide enough for people to talk through. Binational events and social actions—such as over-the-wall volleyball games, vigils, and even yoga classes—sometimes take place across both sides of the border.

One particularly poignant event, Las Posadas, is a Christmastime reenactment of Mary and Joseph's search for shelter on the eve of Jesus' birth. Typically, in Mexico, celebrants will travel to different houses, knocking on doors and asking to be let in, sometimes singing songs. The homeowners will often chant back, "No, there's no room here," and the travelers move on. At the border, this religious ritual takes on a deep resonance. Demonstrations that reenact Las Posadas in Friendship Park reveal the painful lack of hospitality. Mexicans knock on the wall, asking for an invitation, only to be denied.

As Billy and I sat in the somber reality of this ironically named space, everyone on the Mexican side seemed to suddenly stand up and walk toward the fence. It was as if a silent signal had been issued, and now men and women hung on to the diamond-shaped cutouts in the wire fence, staring at the United States. Not one to mind my own business, I followed the crowd and peeked through the holes to view a U.S. parking lot. Car doors slammed, and men, women, and children were walking toward the fence.

Near Billy and me, a Mexican woman with long blond hair stationed a camping chair next to the fence and sat down comfortably. Soon a man on the U.S. side did the same. The woman opened a thermos and squeezed a small Styrofoam cup of coffee to him through a hole in the fence. They sat back and chatted. A few feet away from her, a large family on the U.S. side exclaimed with glee as they grasped at the fingers of Mexican toddlers poking through the small holes.

I gasped. "They're visiting family," I barely whispered to Billy. I felt that I should look away, but I couldn't as I watched hands reach through the fence to grab fingers or give high fives. All the while, Border Patrol idled in the background. I swallowed an audible sob, but tears streamed down my cheeks.

Before long, Billy gently guided me in the direction of our car. This was a sacred time for families, and we felt intrusive.

Just as we began to back out of our parking space, another vehicle pulled in next to us. Three white men hopped out and began unloading professional video and audio equipment. We immediately pulled back into our parking space and sat and watched. One of the men held a microphone in front of the man from the large family. "This is my brother," we heard him say to the rolling cameras. "I have not seen him in five years. This is my first time meeting my nephews. We have brought food to celebrate and eat, but . . ." He gestured toward the fence. "There is no place big enough to pass it."

One videographer stood back from the interview, and I approached him to ask about their project. He explained they were German documentary filmmakers living in Mexico City, and they researching the U.S.-Mexico border. He pointed at the blond woman. "That woman and her husband meet here every Saturday. She can't join him because she can't get papers." I grabbed Billy's hand. A husband and a wife. One who could not get papers legally. Their lives separated by a giant fence. Across razor wire, watchtowers, and expanses of desert, this couple shared an intimate bond and lifelong commitment.

"Why doesn't he just come over and visit?" I asked. I assumed, given the obvious presence of Border Patrol, that the man must not be undocumented. After all, we hadn't gone out late at night or ventured any farther south than L.A. until that green card had arrived. Never would we have set up chairs by the border!

"Good question," the filmmaker said and walked over to talk to the couple. He returned with information that the man was indeed undocumented; crossing into Mexico would mean a perilous journey to return. We gasped. Billy and another on-looker who had joined in our conversation commented on his courage and risk.

I stared at the woman and thought to myself, I just wouldn't do it. If we had been in that situation, I'd have left the United States and lived in Mexico, or in our case, Guatemala. But then I noticed the small blond boy sitting in a miniature camp chair next to his mother. More tears pooled in my eyes. I imagined that husband missed his wife as much as I would have missed Billy. But I suspected the money he sent to her from the United States was raising that child. If he could have done it in Mexico, I imagined he would have done just that.

The documentary filmmaker continued to share about their project, telling me that the film would be viewed in Mexico and in Germany but that it would never be seen in the United States. Billy and I shook our heads in disappointment. "For us," the filmmaker said, "this is the Berlin Wall." He gestured at the fence behind us. "The difference is that there we were clear enemies. Here, the United States and Mexico have free trade, and they are said to be allies, to have a friendly relationship."

His statement lingered in the air as more families arrived at "Friendship Park" on both the U.S. and Mexican sides.

According to BBC News, the new wall that President Trump has promised to build will, in fact, be longer and taller than the since-demolished Berlin Wall.[13] Already, Friendship Park has been transformed from the limited visiting space I witnessed when Billy and I were there. The slats, which previously allowed for a tender touch or small cup of coffee to be passed through them, have now been reinforced with grates that prevent anything larger than a fingertip to connect across the border.

Still, families gather there to have in-person conversations, even if faces are partially obscured. Parents still catch glimpses of the ways their children are growing up and hear the voices of loved ones that will carry them through another week. Mary and Joseph still knock on the door, breathing a prayer that, maybe this time, they will find safety and welcome.

13

BED QUOTA

"Woo hoo!" Billy swooped into our apartment, where I was folding laundry and watching TV. "I found another job," he announced. "It's a different company, same work, but the pay is more than what I was asking Derek for."

"That's great," I told him. "And fast!" He had only decided to look for another job that same morning.

"Yeah, that's just how this industry is. And they know me, know my work. But I told them I want to give Derek two weeks' notice. I think they were kind of surprised, because people don't really do that in construction. But Derek has been good to me, and I don't want to burn any bridges."

It was true that Derek and his wife, with whom he co-owned the company, had appreciated Billy's work. They had even started referring to him as their "son," revealing their affectionate feelings toward him. But the relationship had become awkward a few months earlier when Billy had approached Derek about an overdue raise. Billy's team had handily surpassed multiple production goals, and the raise was in line with what he should expect to be making for work at that level. His boss had agreed. But the next several paychecks came and went without change. Billy followed up. Derek apologized and promised a change in the next check. That Friday, Billy's paycheck was the same, but Derek handed him two tickets to a baseball game.

At the time, we laughed at this apparent "raise." Then came another check, this time accompanied by a digital camera. This uncomfortable saga—combined with other broken promises—had pushed Billy to look for different work.

The day after Billy secured a new job, he went in to give Derek his two weeks' notice. Derek was furious. He screamed in Billy's face. He told him to pack up and go home, and to not even bother finishing out his two weeks. Billy put his vest and helmet inside the work truck and went home. On the way, he called his new employer and told them he could start the next week after all.

We were disappointed in how the situation ended, but we felt Billy had tried to handle it as best he could. Now it was over. Or so we thought.

A few weeks later, Billy ran into a former coworker on his old crew. "Man," Caesar began. "Derek talks about you all the time."

"What?" Billy laughed.

"Yeah, man. He is so mad at you. I've got to tell you. He said he's going to call Immigration and report you. So I'm just giving you a head's up. He's going to try and have you deported, *mano*."

When Billy called and told me this, I couldn't respond. It was true, of course, that when Derek had hired Billy, he had been undocumented—like nearly every other guy on the crew. But that had not been a problem. Until Billy had done something Derek didn't like. Now Billy's status was of paramount importance, and it was a pressure point Derek thought he could push. Since he hadn't told Billy, it didn't seem that he was planning to use it as leverage to get him to return to the company. No. It appeared that Derek was seeking revenge, a punishment to Billy for thinking he was independent.

I exhaled in relief. I was so grateful that Billy was no longer undocumented. Apparently, Derek hadn't noticed when Billy took a few days off for his wedding to an American citizen. And he hadn't paid attention when Billy had asked to leave early for his immigration physical and interview. We realized that Derek didn't know Billy had adjusted his status. We rested easy, knowing any attempts he might make to threaten Billy's presence in the country wouldn't work.

Then Billy received another update from a former coworker still working for Derek. "He called Immigration on you," Trent told Billy. "But they told him you were legal. Man, I've never seen Derek so angry. His face was all red, and he was screaming at everybody. It was crazy."

Billy shook his head. At first, Derek's response had seemed almost amusing. It was unexpected. But now it felt sad and desperate.

I thought again of the network of mutuality Martin Luther King Jr. had spoken of: "We are tied together in the single garment of destiny, caught in an inescapable network of mutuality. And whatever affects one directly affects all indirectly. . . . I can never be what I ought to be until you are what you ought to be. And you can never be what you ought to be until I am what I ought to be."[1] I realized how outdated immigration laws had led to working patterns in which Derek had grown familiar with having full control over his employees. A worker giving his notice had proven to be an offensive affront to Derek's absolute authority.

In that sense, the ongoing delay of immigration reform had a much greater reach than I originally realized. Yes, these outdated laws forced Derek's employees to live and work in the shadows, but they had an effect on Derek too. The dynamic of supervising vulnerable employees had chipped away at his humanity. He had grown accustomed to a level of authority and control that did not honor the mutual dignity of everyone in the workplace. In other words, he was not able to be the full person God created him to be because the men who worked for him were not able to be fully who God created *them* to be.

Former coworkers continued to update Billy on Derek's rage. They said he talked about Billy constantly and asked the guys if anyone was keeping in touch with him. We weren't sure what to do. We assumed everything would blow over, though we did feel a twinge of unease. Then a couple of months after he'd started at his new job, Billy was called into the office.

"Hi, Billy," his new boss, Tommy, began. "So we got a call from your old boss today. Derek?"

"Uh-huh," Billy nodded, bracing himself for whatever was about to come.

"Yeah, well, he's telling us that you're illegal and you don't have the proper papers to be working here?"

Billy reached for his wallet. "When I started working for Derek, there was a problem with my paperwork," he confessed. "But about a year ago, I got married. My wife is a U.S. citizen, and we were able to go through the legal process to get everything adjusted. I have a valid driver's license." He set it on the desk. "And I can bring my Social Security card tomorrow if you want to see it. I don't keep it on me."

Tommy picked up the license and turned it over in his hand. "Yeah . . ." He drew out the word as he slid the ID back to Billy. "I mean, I believe you. But Derek is saying he's going to call the companies we contract for and tell them our lead supervisor is illegal. These are big-name companies, with reputations to protect. We'll lose the work if they're worried that they're knowingly giving work to illegals."

"But I'm not illegal," Billy protested. "I mean, I was, but I'm not anymore. By the time you hired me, I had all my paperwork in order."

"Yeah," Tommy sighed, and leaned back. "But these companies aren't going to start checking into their subcontractors' documents to confirm. Derek is stirring up controversy around you, and it's easier for them just to give the work to a different contractor and avoid the hassle and people looking into it, you know?"

"Yeah, no. I know." Billy picked up his driver's license and pushed it back into his wallet.

"So I don't think we're going to be able to assign you to any more work for a while," Tommy said, avoiding eye contact. "At least until this dies down. Maybe we can touch base next week?"

Billy nodded. "Go ahead and head home," Tommy said. "We'll pay you for today."

Billy was angry and frustrated. He'd tried to do the right thing. Fix his papers. Communicate with his employer. Give two weeks' notice. But Derek still seemed to hold the power, and his capacity to hold a grudge had extended months beyond what we thought was possible. We grew concerned about just how far Derek might take his anger toward Billy.

And now this new employer, and the parent company holding the contracts, preferred to wash their hands of the matter rather than stand up for Billy. We understood their desire not to "open that can of worms," but it felt hopeless for us as we tried to make our way and pay our bills.

Eventually, Billy and Tommy figured out a creative way to affirm Billy's legal status and work around Derek's vengeful attacks. Before long, he was back out on the worksite, this time wearing a name tag that used his full first name rather than his nickname ("Billy") and his mother's last name instead of his father's. Like many Latinos, Billy's legal name included both parents' surnames. He had come out of the shadows, but he still had to figure out how to navigate an immigration system that corrupts and exploits.

I sometimes wonder what would have happened if Billy had been detained and deported. Our entire experience of marriage and living as a mixed-status family had felt isolating and confusing. But we'd always found resources and people to help guide us through that process. I knew absolutely nothing about how immigrants were detained and deported. The whole system seemed shrouded in mystery.

But many years later, I would learn more about U.S. detention centers, and I would see how differently our life could have looked if Derek had gotten his way and had Billy deported. After we left Los Angeles and moved to Atlanta, I found myself sitting in the visitation room of one of the largest immigration detention centers in the United States.

* * *

My knees bounced slightly under the table in front of me. Even though I was in a row of five folding chairs, the partitions separating us made me feel alone in the windowless room. In front of me, a thick glass window rose from the table to the ceiling. An empty chair sat on the other side, soon to be filled by a man wearing a red or blue jumpsuit and carrying an ID badge. Together, we would pick up telephones on our respective sides of the glass and talk.

Located in a rural county in Georgia, Stewart Detention Center houses over 1,700 men who have been detained, primarily in the Southeast.[2] But others are transferred from states as far away as our former home in California. Immigrants detained in the facility had requested visitors from El Refugio, a local hospitality ministry that offers support and housing to family members visiting detainees and that coordinates volunteers to visit other detainees as well. Members of our Atlanta-based church had responded to those requests for visitors. We'd loaded up the church van early one Saturday and driven more than two hours to the facility, where we were given the name of one man who'd requested a visit. We were treated the same as visiting friends and family—security checks, no cell phones, hours of waiting, and endless protocol. El Refugio managed the visits carefully to make sure we weren't accidentally hijacking a detainee's one weekly visit if an actual friend or relative was there to see him.

I looked at the glass and noticed several small handprints a few feet above my head. I imagined a small child standing on the table and pressing her hands—and probably her face—to the

El Refugio offers meals and a place for families to stay when they visit detainees at Stewart Detention Center in Lumpkin, Georgia.

window. She had wanted to touch someone she loved, someone who would likely soon be deported.

According to the Southern Poverty Law Center, immigrants held in Georgia detention centers are more likely to face deportation than detainees in other states. The national deportation rate was around 60 percent in the 2015 fiscal year, but Stewart deported over 87 percent of its detainees.[3] Many detainees were nonviolent offenders whose only charge was their unlawful entry to the United States. This is a misdemeanor offense, such as speeding or driving without a license. Charges can be escalated to felony status if a person was previously deported and has reentered the States unlawfully. Others in detention in Stewart were like Billy, people who entered legally and overstayed their visas. This violation of federal immigration law, though not a misdemeanor or a felony, can also result in deportation. Others at Stewart had previously fulfilled a U.S. prison sentence for a crime committed in the States and had been transferred to await removal from the country.

Detainees at Stewart live in a medium-security prison privately owned and operated by Corrections Corporation of America (CCA), which recently rebranded as CoreCivic, a private prison corporation that runs for-profit prisons and detention centers across the country. The federal prison population has boomed in the last few decades. To deal with the surge in inmates, the federal government began outsourcing to private companies such as CCA. In August 2016, U.S. deputy attorney general Sally Yates announced a gradual phasing-out of the federal government's use of private prisons. She instructed the Bureau of Prisons to analyze these contracts as they came up for renewal and to either end them or reduce their scope.[4] In March 2017, however, attorney general Jeff Sessions reversed this decision.[5]

In any case, however, this memorandum did not apply to immigration detention, which provides profits for the same corporations. According to *U.S. News and World Report*, more than 70 percent of detained immigrants were held in private facilities in 2016.[6] Detention centers can be very profitable for companies. Because they do not share the goal of reintegration back into American society, they often are not required to offer the same programs that prisons are. In addition, these facilities benefit from the fact that Immigration and Customs Enforcement (ICE), which apprehends immigrant offenders, is congressionally mandated to detain an average of 34,000 immigrants nightly.[7] This practice, also referred to as the "bed quota," means that, in some ways, it doesn't matter how immigration trends ebb and flow. The bed quota protects the bottom line of the corporations running the detention centers while also guaranteeing a minimum transfer of federal dollars to those private companies. In turn, ICE is expected to maintain this nightly average of 34,000 detainees. It is the only law enforcement agency in the country to have this type of mandate.[8]

The federal government spends approximately $164 a day to detain each immigrant. Given the bed quota, this adds up to over $5 million a day to hold immigrants in detention facilities.[9]

Billy visited a detainee at another window a bit further down the row from me. When we exited the prison and returned to the glaring sunlight, Billy looked at the ground. "He was so much like me," Billy said to me, his voice weak. "Our stories were almost the same. We've been to some of the same places. And he's a dad like me." I saw Billy's eyes water as he thought about being separated from our two children. "I never realized I could end up in a place like this." He gestured toward the facility we'd just exited.

I couldn't disagree. We had both assumed that if he'd ever been detained, he would be deported quickly. That somehow he would communicate his whereabouts to me and then I'd go join him in Guatemala. It wasn't our ideal plan, of course, but it had felt like a manageable plan B. But the man I'd visited with had been in detention for seven months and had no idea as to the status of his case or when he might be deported or released. It was sobering to realize that Billy could have been transported and held anywhere in the country, without the basic rights granted to U.S. citizens, and with an unknown wait ahead of him.

Immigration and detention systems can be overwhelming for families with a loved one being held. Language barriers, fears of engaging the detention system for family members who may also be undocumented, and the everyday challenges of adjusting to a new culture and a new country's justice system can present real hurdles. And many families are navigating this system alone. Many of the men our group talked to did not have legal representation. Immigrants are not afforded public defenders, as is required by law for U.S. citizens. Therefore many of them represent themselves. And though the practice has been criticized, even children are not guaranteed counsel and may represent themselves in immigration court. One judge went so far as to say that three- and four-year-olds are capable of navigating the justice system on their own.[10]

In the face of such a daunting injustice, it's easy to feel discouraged and nearly listless. Personally, I feel intimidated by the web of inadequate immigration laws, the need for skilled lawyers and other professionals, and the privatization of immigration detention centers. How do we as people of faith respond?

I have been encouraged and inspired by the work of El Refugio, the hospitality ministry that organized our visit. This innovative nonprofit rents a house in Lumpkin, the small town that is home to Stewart Detention Center. Since Lumpkin has no hotels and only two restaurants, El Refugio offers a haven for families—many of whom have traveled across state lines— while visiting a loved one in detention. El Refugio offers a free place to sleep and a well-stocked fridge. Many of these visitors come to see their family's primary breadwinner, who is now in detention. Volunteers at El Refugio welcome these families and offer care and comfort to them during their stay.

In addition, El Refugio manages pen pal programs for detainees who write letters and desire a response from the world outside detention. Before our visit, our congregation had mailed Father's Day cards to men in the center. Though it was difficult to find the right words to encourage fathers separated from their children, we wanted to acknowledge their invaluable role in their families. El Refugio receives letters from detainees in English, Spanish, French, Chinese, and more languages, and they recruit volunteers fluent in these languages to write back and foster an ongoing relationship. And for the detainees who request visitors, El Refugio organizes groups to go to the center and meet with them to simply talk and visit.

El Refugio is an uncomplicated ministry of hospitality alongside the complex issue of immigration detention. Jesus said, "I was in prison and you came to me" (Matthew 25:36). Jesus is intimately familiar with the justice system. In his life on earth, he was on trial, convicted, and put to death. He is not far from those suffering behind bars, and he invites us to visit.

We debriefed with our church members after the visit, and congregants were moved to tears as we all shared how we'd seen both ourselves and the image of God in the faces and stories of the detainees.

Detention is an isolating experience in every sense of the word—from the rural location of the facility to the disconnection from friends and family to the loneliness of incarceration and navigating one's legal situation. When the letters requesting visits arrive, we cannot assume an "out of sight, out of mind" posture. Jesus reminds us, "Truly, I say to you, as you did it to one of the least of these my brothers, you did it to me" (Matthew 25:40).

When I think about brothers and sisters in detention, I want to be like the little child whose handprints I saw on the detention center window. I want to stand up tall, press my hands and face to the glass, and look for Jesus on the other side.

14

CITIZENSHIP WITHOUT BORDERS

I held my newborn son in the doctor's office after his two-week checkup. We were waiting for final instructions before checking out when my phone rang. I saw Billy's smiling face on the caller ID.

I juggled the baby and adjusted the diaper bag slung over my shoulder, trying to answer before it went to voicemail. "Hello?" I breathed, eager and excited. While I'd been discussing feeding frequencies and numbers of wet diapers, Billy had been recalling details about constitutional amendments and historical wars. He was taking his U.S. citizenship test.

"How did it go?" I asked, almost holding my breath.

"I passed!" he said, and I could hear him smiling through the phone. I whooped in celebration. I'd known he knew the information backward and forward, but he'd been frantically studying for months, convinced that he didn't quite have it down pat. He had also been nervous about the timing of his test. We'd had no say in the scheduling of his appointment, so when the letter arrived announcing it would be just twelve days after our son's due date, we were concerned.

Our older daughter had showed up on the scene ten days late, and she and I had both stayed in the hospital for five days. If our son had followed the same path, I'd have been eating lemon sorbet alone while Billy left us at the hospital to go take this test. It wasn't our ideal scenario. But second babies march to their own drums, and so I was at the doctor's office with a bubbly newborn while Billy was wowing the U.S. government with his English proficiency and civics knowledge.

After Billy had been a legal permanent resident (also known as an LPR) for five years, he became eligible to apply for naturalized U.S. citizenship. The main difference between being a legal permanent resident and a citizen is the right to vote, but it also includes other changes like eligibility to serve on a jury, the opportunity to obtain a U.S. passport, and the freedom to leave the country for more than six months without questioning or a reentry process. Many people remain legal permanent residents for their lifetime. In fact, the Pew Research Center notes that in 2011, almost 10 million immigrants who were eligible for naturalization had not yet naturalized. More than a third of these eligible citizens (3.5 million) are originally from Mexico.[1]

Billy was passionate about becoming a citizen. First of all, his wife and two children were all U.S. citizens, and he had made his home here. Additionally, after years of working and living alongside undocumented immigrants, he knew firsthand the need for immigration reform. He felt convicted that ignoring the opportunity to vote would be like leaving his brothers behind now that his own situation was resolved. And he also admitted his concern that if the laws changed one day, his permanent residence could be uncertain. I assured him that could never happen.

But I may have been wrong. On January 27, 2017, President Trump signed an executive order banning U.S. entrance for travelers from Iran and six other majority-Muslim countries. Initially, legal permanent residents of the United States whose country of origin was one of those named were also barred from reentering the States. One Iranian citizen, describing his concern in an interview with NPR, wondered about the security of his own legal permanent residence. "What if I happened to be outside of the country and wanted to come back?" he said. "This is home. I mean, I own a house here. I have no other place to go."[2]

The White House later released a statement exempting legal residents from the travel restrictions. But the initial confusion shook up many documented immigrants in the United States and created a surge in applications for citizenship. In fact, the Coalition for Humane Immigrant Rights of Los Angeles, or CHIRLA, began offering free assistance during Trump's first hundred days in office. Their director of communications, Jorge-Mario Cabrera, told NPR, "We used to see two to three people a week seeking citizenship services. Now we are seeing between thirty and fifty people a day."[3]

* * *

"Will there be any kind of ceremony or anything?" I asked Billy.

"Yes, well . . ." He hesitated. "It's actually today at two thirty, if you think you could make it?" I hesitated while figuring out logistics, but I already knew I would be there. I packed up my scattered belongings, which managed to give the appearance that my son and I had temporarily moved into the exam room. (How can babies so small come with so many accessories?)

I typed the unfamiliar address into the GPS and headed toward the suburbs of Atlanta. I had envisioned a grandiose auditorium—like a college graduation ceremony, but with the world's flags lined up on the stage. Instead, we pulled into a nondescript office complex not far from the interstate. I fed my son in the car before we shuffled into the government building to celebrate my husband's induction into the United States of America.

Even as I walked through the door, I was aware of all the ways in which our lives could have turned out differently. What if I'd walked away when Billy told me about his status? What if we hadn't been able to replace Billy's lost document and been required to move to Guatemala? What if we hadn't had the resources to go through the application process? What if Billy's boss had been successful in having him deported?

There are a thousand different plotlines in the story of immigration. And we knew dozens of different scenarios had been possible for us. But we had landed in the one that led here, to this North Atlanta office complex.

* * *

Had we gotten married before 1940, Billy could not have gained citizenship through his U.S.-born wife. In fact, at that time in history, marrying Billy would have required *me* to give up my U.S. citizenship. The Expatriation Act of 1907 declared that "any American woman who marries a foreigner shall take the nationality of her husband."[4]

Not only that, but I may have been seen by some as disloyal to my country, something akin to a traitor. In the early 1900s, citizens were worried about the influx of immigrants from eastern and southern Europe. (Notice a pattern in our country's history?) Historian Candice Lewis Bredbenner writes in her book, *A Nationality of Her Own*, that "a citizen woman's marriage to a foreigner became vulnerable to interpretation as a brazenly un-American act."[5]

But one woman was not having it. In 1915, Ethel MacKenzie, a U.S. citizen whose husband was from Great Britain, contested the law all the way to the Supreme Court.[6] She claimed that if the law was intended to apply to her—a U.S.-born woman who remained living in the States with a resident foreigner—then it was beyond the authority of Congress. She leveraged past precedents to argue that a citizen could not be "denationalized" without his or her consent unless being punished for a crime.

MacKenzie lost her case, and the court defined her situation as voluntary expatriation. Essentially, since the law said that women lose their citizenship when they marry a foreigner, she had made the decision to marry despite the known consequence, and therefore Congress wasn't taking her citizenship from her. She had given it up. In other words, the court said, "You knew what you were getting into!"

It's important to note that U.S. men who married foreign women did not suffer the same consequence. In fact, in those international couplings, the woman *automatically* received U.S. citizenship. It's also critical to recognize that the Expatriation Act was passed—in this hypocritical way—when only men had the right to vote. Once women won the right to vote in 1920, they immediately went to work and lobbied for the Cable Act, which was passed in 1922.[7] This legislation allowed a U.S. woman to maintain her citizenship if she married a foreign man who was eligible to gain U.S. citizenship, even if he chose not to. (This fine print regarding eligibility primarily excluded women who married Chinese immigrants, as they were not allowed to gain U.S. citizenship.)

Thankfully, by 1940, the remaining restrictions were removed, clearing the pathway for me to maintain my own citizenship and even open the door for Billy to obtain U.S. citizenship as well. But one glaring truth, evident to me in this historical timeline, is how the world is motivated by its own interests. When men were the only ones voting, they made sure they kept their own citizenship regardless of marriage. Once women began voting, they won that right for themselves. Laws are designed from the perspective of and for the interests of those in power.

* * *

Worrying only about ourselves may be our natural bent as humans. Do we have enough? Are we getting all the good things we deserve? Are our kids getting the best of everything the world has to offer? Are we protected? Are we safe? Are we keeping up with the Joneses? Will we have enough in the future? Will our kids have enough?

But this approach to life—this obsession with our own interests—is damaging on a collective level and exhausting on a personal one. Collectively, laws that benefit only a select, powerful group can easily turn to exploit, abuse, and crush those not part of that group. And on a personal level, preoccupation with our own interests is, well, exhausting. Our own interests will deplete us of our energy, resources, community, and ultimately, our humanity.

But fear not! There is good news. In the gospel of Matthew, Jesus tells us, "Do not be anxious, saying, 'What shall we eat?' or 'What shall we drink?' or 'What shall we wear?' For the Gentiles seek after all these things, and your heavenly Father knows that you need them all. But seek first the kingdom of God and his righteousness, and all these things will be added to you" (Matthew 6:31-33).

The Gentiles seek after all these things. It is no surprise to God that we worry about what we'll be eating, drinking, and wearing. It is human nature to worry about one's own interests. It doesn't surprise God when we worry about our jobs or crime rates or unfamiliar languages. Our human nature is to put ourselves first.

But God doesn't allow us to stay in this self-focused place. We are challenged to reconsider how we think about others. I love how Eugene Peterson paraphrases these verses from Philippians in *The Message*:

> If you've gotten anything at all out of following Christ, if his love has made any difference in your life, if being in a community of the Spirit means anything to you, if you have a heart, if you *care*—then do me a favor: Agree with each other, love each other, be deep-spirited friends. Don't push your way to the front; don't sweet-talk your way to the top. Put yourself aside, and help others get ahead. Don't be obsessed with getting your own advantage. Forget yourselves long enough to lend a helping hand. (Philippians 2:1-4)

We cannot stay hidden in our proverbial staircases, peeking out from self-constructed bunkers and worrying for our own needs and safety. What if we trusted God to feed us like the birds and clothe us like the flowers (Matthew 6:26-28) and used our energy to make sure others' needs are met? What if we turned away from fear of the unfamiliar and got to work helping our immigrant neighbors flourish?

As a child, I listened to a sermon illustration in which someone travels between heaven and hell. This supernatural commuter stops for lunch in hell's dining hall, where hordes of people push in around long tables for bowls of soup. (I can barely eat tortilla soup in Atlanta summers, so this seems like exactly what you'd be served in a fiery hell.) The bigger problem is that everyone has a spoon tied to their hand that is twice the length of their arm. So while they can scoop the soup, no one can transfer the food from their spoon to their mouth. There is shouting and complaining and general gnashing of teeth.

Then our tour guide beams out of the netherworld and pops into heaven's mess hall, where, as it turns out, everyone also has soup and the same giant spoons strapped to their arms. (There must've been a supernatural sale!) But the traveler immediately notices that chaos is absent and that everyone is enjoying their meal. As it turns out, they are each feeding the person across from themselves. In doing so, all are fed.

* * *

We are familiar with the shouting and complaining and gnashing of teeth. We're living in the midst of it every day. And immigration is most certainly a topic that brings tension and anger bubbling to the surface. It's a complicated, multifaceted issue that affects people from all over the world and in every corner of the United States.

But when we view others as encroaching on our resources, our neighborhoods, or our way of life, we miss out. We are tempted to draw thick lines around what is "ours" or who is "in." But God has invited us into a larger story. It's a story of redemption and restoration, of being rescued from our own selfish absorption and ambition. It's a story in which we don't have to strive to be the hero. We can trust God's Word that our needs are known and will be added unto us as we seek God's kingdom.

God has welcomed us into an expansive family and offered us citizenship in a kingdom that knows no borders. In this kingdom, our allegiance is to God alone. We look to Jesus' example to reach across society's lines to the marginalized and oppressed, and we seek to follow God above any human ruler.

Conversation on immigration in the United States is changing weekly. Legislation has been introduced to cut legal immigration in half.[8] Refugee resettlement programs have been paused. At the time of this writing, the fate of the Dreamers—undocumented young adults who were brought to the United States as children and who have grown up here—hangs in the balance. And it's not out of the realm of possibility that Christian acts of hospitality, such as offering rides or serving meals, could become questionable or illegal in our time. It's difficult to know

Billy and I and our children participated in a public witness at the Atlanta airport in 2017.

exactly where immigration policy will go in the future. But it's not difficult to know that whenever our allegiance to God is at odds with the state, we are committed to following God. Loving our neighbor, welcoming the stranger, showing hospitality to our brothers and sisters draws us closer to the heart of the gospel and to the people made in God's image.

The beauty of being part of the wide and diverse family of God is the variety of roles we are invited to play. There is no singular Christian response to immigration. Goodness knows I sometimes wish that there was. I like a schedule, a plan, a five-step checklist to make it all work better. But we do not need to be paralyzed by the complexity of the system. In fact, the countless needs means there are plenty of unique opportunities for Christ-followers of all gifts and skills to participate. Immigration may continue to be complicated, but loving our neighbor can be simple.

I believe relationships are the starting place for meaningful work. Our friendships grow deeper and more authentic over time. And as we all sit at the expansive family table, we bring our diverse skills and interests to share. For some, that looks like small, concrete works of mercy for the immigrant next door: inviting someone over for tea, helping a parent fill out elementary school paperwork, or driving a neighbor to the doctor. For others, it may look like macro-level work of law and advocacy: defending immigrants in court, organizing marches and political actions, running for office.

There are countless opportunities for every Christ-follower to stand alongside immigrants. It may be welcoming into family or church children whose parents have been deported. Or visiting men, women, and children locked in immigrant detention. It may be paying for the college education of a young immigrant adult who has been accepted into a school but is ineligible for scholarships. It may be participating in marches and letter-writing campaigns. It may be fostering unaccompanied minors awaiting court proceedings, teaching English to new arrivals, preparing apartments for refugee families, or opening our church as a place of sanctuary for those in need of safety. The list is endless.

As we have reflected on our experiences, Billy and I have felt compelled to support and advocate for immigrant families. Billy sensed a deep desire to create sustainable jobs in Guatemala. He'd witnessed how lack of opportunity took away choice for families who immigrated to the United States. And we also know how difficult it is for deportees returning to the country to find work. In 2017, Billy started meeting with local Guatemalan leaders and interested U.S. supporters. Together, we started work on Bridge, an organization that creates jobs in Guatemala to promote dignity and opportunity for Guatemalan families and deportees.[9]

U.S. citizens, undocumented immigrants, legal permanent residents, documented immigrants: we are all welcome in the kingdom family of God. As we live in this broken world, we pray together, "Your kingdom come, your will be done, on earth as it is in heaven" (Matthew 6:10). We can pick up our ridiculously long spoons and serve each other, setting aside our own fears and self-interests. Living in the absence of fear and the saturation of love is a witness to a different way of life that can only have been inspired by Jesus' example. Together we can catch glimpses of God's kingdom here on earth.

* * *

I found Billy waiting to be led into the room for the naturalization ceremony. Together, we filed in with the 120 other immigrants also celebrating this important milestone. Maybe I should have noticed I was the only nonimmigrant in this line. But I was in the exhausted fog of new motherhood and clinging to a two-week-old baby with a tiny rock-star faux hawk. No one said anything as I sat down with the newly minted citizens rather than in the section for friends and family. By the time I realized my mistake, there was no going back.

For almost six years, we'd been receiving letters from U.S. Citizenship and Immigration Services. Every piece of snail mail was highly anticipated, and each one succinctly communicated our next steps: "We received your application. You'll hear from us soon." "Appear at this time and at this place to be fingerprinted." "Your interview has been scheduled." "Please keep this letter for your records." "Appear at this time and place to be fingerprinted" (again).

The good news along the way had been shared in the same manner: "Congratulations. Here is your work permit." "Congratulations. You are a legal permanent resident." Official letters worth more to us than gold could have been lost in the mail. The whole process had felt that fragile.

A woman stood behind a podium and welcomed the crowd. She began to list the fifty countries represented in the room of immigrants. The array of faces and families around me was awe-inspiring. Such a stunning gathering of people made in God's image from all over the world. I wanted to know their stories. The couple from Indonesia sitting in front of us with their two children. The Indian woman next to me. The family behind us who cheered the loudest when Colombia was called.

"I know you've worked really hard to get to this place," the officiant said. "This is a really big accomplishment, and we are here to celebrate." Without warning, tears began rolling down my cheeks. I had never thought of becoming a citizen as an accomplishment. For so long, it hadn't seemed that there was a clear end in sight. Instead, we put one foot in front of the other: filling out the next piece of paperwork, signing the cashier's checks, doing whatever it took to move our family forward through the process. The woman's acknowledgment of the challenge, the waiting, and the relief pricked my heart and unlocked my tears.

This is a big deal, I thought. I didn't know anyone in that room besides Billy and our son, but I felt a deep kinship with the others who were there, knowing we had all experienced something similar. I knew that some had walked a relatively straightforward line into that room. Others had experienced heartbreak and demonstrated resilience that I'd never be able to imagine. Still others were outside this room, waiting and wishing that they, too, could be welcomed as full participants in the country they call home.

We had come a long way. When we'd started dating, I thought Billy would need a half day off work. Instead, we'd walked through six years, three addresses, two states, and two kids to arrive in this room. Every piece of mail, every appointment, every shred of paperwork had been confusing, stressful, and overwhelming. But where the immigration system had tried to swallow me whole, one thing had always been amazingly simple: loving the guy sitting next to me.

ACKNOWLEDGMENTS

Southern girls are committed to thank-you notes, and I am deeply grateful to all those who made *Love Undocumented* a reality. A big shout-out to my editor, Valerie Weaver-Zercher, who made this book better in a thousand different ways and was committed to the message from the very beginning. Thanks to everyone at Herald Press for such wonderful support along the way.

We wouldn't have a story to tell if it weren't for those who walked with us in the early, awkward days of our relationship. Sarah Houser, thank you for learning to drive stick shift so we could go and meet Los Angeles together. Ellen Hume, I'm always grateful to you and Rich for welcoming me into your home, church, and life. Juan and Stacie Paz, would Billy and I have ever even met if it weren't for you? Lauren Tigrett and Sarah Ahn, thank you for going with me to Guatemala, meeting my future in-laws, and not laughing too hard when they asked if I loved Billy and I changed the subject. Thank you, Danny Martinez, and Kevin and Jen Blue, for supporting us and pastoring us so graciously in the early years of our marriage.

I am forever indebted to amazing friends who have walked with me through the ups and downs of the publishing journey, and whose encouragement almost always involved coffee or tacos. Thank you, Becca Stanley, Michelle Acker Perez, Laura Pritchard-Compton, Katie Delp, Ashlee Starr, Melissa Cazorla, and Frances Coleman: for reading chapters, Voxing me when I was panicking that writing means spending time alone, and sending notes, prayers, and incredible GIFs. You all are the best! To Shannan Martin, Osheta Moore, Marie Marquardt, Jim Dudley, D. L. Mayfield, and Eugene Cho: thank you for the ways you made space and supported me in this project. To Leroy Barber, Anton Flores-Maisonet, Paul and Young Lee Hertig, and Matthew Soerens: thank you for all you have taught me about solidarity with the poor and understanding immigration in this country.

I cannot say thank you enough to our families: the Quezadas, Dominguezes, Dotterweichs, and Brooks. You all have showed us what it looks like to open your life and home and welcome in new folks as family. Thank you, Mom and Dad, for all the ways you have cheered me on, from elementary basketball and after-dinner dance performances to moving to the city and writing this book. To Lucky, who eight years after our wedding finally received her tourist visa: thank you for coming to Atlanta and hanging out with my kids while I wrote this book. And to Cuty: thank you for always showing me such love. My cough is doing much better.

Thank you, thank you, thank you to all those who have shared with me your own immigration stories and challenges. My heart has stayed tender and my resolve has grown deeper because of you, your resilience, your passion, and your courage. You are important to God's kingdom, and you are valuable in our world today. We will keep on working to welcome and make room at the table for all God's children.

And of course, my people. Gabriella, thank you for offering to do the illustrations for this book. Your enthusiasm and heart for others inspires me. Isaac, thanks for all the hugs when I was out writing so much. Your sweetness is an encouragement. And thank you, Billy, for laughing at my jokes, asking me to marry you, trusting me with your story, and supporting this book one thousand percent. You are a rock star!

NOTES

1 Stairwells and Bunkers

1 "Westlake Profile," Mapping L.A., *Los Angeles Times*, June 2009, accessed July 11, 2017, http://maps.latimes.com/neighborhoods/ neighborhood/westlake/.

2 Ibid.

3 Jie Zong and Jeanne Batalova, "Frequently Requested Statistics on Immigrants and Immigration in the United States," Migration Policy Institute, March 8, 2017, http://www.migrationpolicy.org/article/ frequently-requested-statistics-immigrants-and-immigration -united-states.

4 Ali Noorani, *There Goes the Neighborhood: How Communities Overcome Prejudice and Meet the Challenge of American Immigration* (Amherst: Prometheus Books, 2017), 30.

5 LifeWay Research, *Evangelical Views on Immigration*, February 2015, 16, http://lifewayresearch.com/wp-content/uploads/ 2015/03/Evangelical-Views-on-Immigration-Report.pdf.

6 Shane Claiborne, *The Irresistible Revolution* (Grand Rapids, MI: Zondervan, 2006), 113.

7 Patrick Sisson, "Bunkered Down: Shelters, Safe Rooms, and Designing for an Age of Anxiety," *Curbed*, November 2, 2016, https://www.curbed.com/2016/11/2/13479430/ bunker-panic-room-home-anxiety.

8 Ibid.

9 Ibid.

2 Coffee with a Rock Star

1 Christopher Ingraham, "Three Quarters of Whites Don't Have Any Non-White Friends," *Washington Post*, August 25, 2014, https://www.washingtonpost.com/news/wonk/wp/2014/08/25/three-quarters-of-whites-dont-have-any-non-white-friends/?utm_term=.b7c72ae0d7d9.

2 Find out more about Mission Year at https://missionyear.org.

3 Illegal

1 LifeWay Research, *Evangelical Views on Immigration*, February 2015, 16, http://lifewayresearch.com/wp-content/uploads/2015/03/Evangelical-Views-on-Immigration-Report.pdf.

2 Amy Clark, "Is NAFTA Good for Mexico's Farmers?" CBS News, July 1, 2006, http://www.cbsnews.com/news/is-nafta-good-for-mexicos-farmers/.

3 Ana Arana, "The New Battle for Central America," *Foreign Affairs* 80, no. 6 (November/December 2001), https://www.foreignaffairs.com/articles/central-america-caribbean/2001-11-01/new-battle-central-america.

4 Alexia Salvatierra, interview with author, March 7, 2017.

5 Meghan Twohey, et al., "Brokers Recruiting Foreign Workers for U.S. Firms Compound Abuses," Reuters, February 19, 2016, http://www.reuters.com/article/us-workers-brokers/brokers-recruiting-foreign-workers-for-u-s-firms-compound-abuses-idUSKCN0VS1XU.

6 "Attorney General Jeff Sessions Delivers Remarks before Media Availability in El Paso, Texas," U.S. Department of Justice, updated April 20, 2017, https://www.justice.gov/opa/speech/attorney-general-jeff-sessions-delivers-remarks-media-availability-el-paso-texas.

7 Michelle Mark and Diana Yukari, "'Wait Your Turn': The Incredibly Complicated Process behind Legal Immigration to the US," *Business Insider*, April 28, 2017, http://www.businessinsider

.com/how-to-green-card-visa-legal-immigration-us-news-trump
-2017-4.

8 "The Current Immigration Process: Why Don't They Just
Immigrate the Legal Way?" G92, accessed May 19, 2017, http://g92
.org/find-answers/process/.

9 "United States Border Patrol Southwest Family Unit Subject and
Unaccompanied Alien Children Apprehensions Fiscal Year 2016:
Statement by Secretary Johnson on Southwest Border Security," U.S.
Customs and Border Protection, October 18, 2016, https://www.cbp
.gov/newsroom/stats/southwest-border-unaccompanied-children/
fy-2016.

10 Ibid.

11 Manny Fernandez, "A Path to America, Marked by More and
More Bodies," *New York Times*, May 4, 2017, https://www.nytimes
.com/interactive/2017/05/04/us/texas-border-migrants-dead-bodies
.html.

12 For an accessible book and the story of one such Central
American migrant, see Sonia Nazario, *Enrique's Journey: The Story
of a Boy's Dangerous Odyssey to Reunite with His Mother* (New York:
Random House, 2007).

13 Mark Krikorian, "On Immigration, Fighting the Last War,"
National Review, October 1, 2015, http://www.nationalreview.com/
article/424879/immigration-fighting-last-war-mark-krikorian.

14 Robert Warren and Donald Kerwin, "Beyond DAPA and
DACA: Revisiting Legislative Reform in Light of Long-Term Trends
in Unauthorized Immigration to the United States," *Journal on
Migration and Human Security* 3, no. 1 (2015): 81, https://
doi.org/10.14240/jmhs.v3i1.45.

15 Alison Siskin, Andorra Bruno, Blas Nunez-Neto, Lisa M.
Seghetti, and Ruth Ellen Wasem, *Immigration Enforcement within
the United States*, U.S. Congressional Research Service (RL33351,
April 6, 2006), 8, http://immigration.procon.org/sourcefiles/
ImmigrationEnforcementWithintheUnitedStates.pdf.

16 Krikorian, "On Immigration."

17 Jeffrey S. Passel and D'Vera Cohn, "Homeland Security Produces
First Estimate of Foreign Visitors to U.S. Who Overstay Deadline to
Leave," Pew Research Center, February 3, 2016, http://www
.pewresearch.org/fact-tank/2016/02/03/homeland-security-produces

-first-estimate-of-foreign-visitors-to-u-s-who-overstay-deadline-to
-leave/. Overstays by country of origin were Canada: 93,035; Mexico:
42,114; Brazil: 35,707; Germany: 21,394; Italy: 17,661; United
Kingdom: 16,446.

18 U.S. Department of Homeland Security, *Entry/Exit Overstay
Report: Fiscal Year 2015*, January 19, 2016, 5, https://www
.dhs.gov/sites/default/files/publications/FY%2015%20DHS%20
Entry%20and%20Exit%20Overstay%20Report.pdf.

4 Coyote Inn

1 "Inside the Hidden World of Immigrant Smuggling," NPR's *Talk
of the Nation*, April 19, 2012, http://www.npr.org/2012/04/19/
150973748/inside-the-hidden-world-of-immigrant-smuggling.

2 Catherine Rampell, "Why Are Mexican Smugglers' Fees Still
Rising?" *Economix* (blog), *New York Times*, May 18, 2009, https://
economix.blogs.nytimes.com/2009/05/18/the-rise-in-mexican
-smugglers-fees/.

3 "Inside the Hidden World," *Talk of the Nation*.

4 "Human Trafficking and Smuggling," U.S. Immigration and
Customs Enforcement, last modified January 16, 2013, https://www
.ice.gov/factsheets/human-trafficking.

5 "Statistics on Forced Labour, Modern Slavery and Human
Trafficking," International Labour Organization, accessed July 22,
2017, http://www.ilo.org/global/topics/forced-labour/policy-areas/
statistics/lang--en/index.htm.

6 Jeffrey S. Passel and D'Vera Cohn, *Size of U.S. Unauthorized
Immigrant Workforce Stable after the Great Recession*, Pew Research
Center, November 3, 2016, 14–15, http://assets
.pewresearch.org/wp-content/uploads/sites/7/2016/11/02160338/
LaborForce2016_FINAL_11.2.16-1.pdf.

7 Ibid., 16.

8 Ibid., 33–34.

9 Ibid., 14.

10 Ibid., 26, 30.

11 Sarah Maslin Nir, "The Price of Nice Nails," *New York Times*,
May 7, 2015, https://www.nytimes.com/2015/05/10/nyregion/at-nail
-salons-in-nyc-manicurists-are-underpaid-and-unprotected.html.

12 Harold Meyerson, "Protecting Undocumented Workers," *Los Angeles Times*, June 24, 2011, http://articles.latimes.com/2011/jun/24/opinion/la-oe-meyerson-undocumented-abuses-20110624.

5 Red Flags

1 Diane Guerrero, *In the Country We Love: My Family Divided* (New York: Henry Holt, 2016), 29–32, 68.

2 NPR Staff, "A Reagan Legacy: Amnesty for Illegal Immigrants," NPR's *All Things Considered*, July 4, 2010, http://www.npr.org/templates/story/story.php?storyId=128303672.

3 "Consideration of Deferred Action for Childhood Arrivals (DACA)," U.S. Citizenship and Immigration Services (archive), accessed July 2017, https://www.uscis.gov/archive/consideration-deferred-action-childhood-arrivals-daca.

4 Los Angeles Times Staff, "Transcript: Donald Trump's Full Immigration Speech, Annotated," *Los Angeles Times*, August 31, 2016, http://www.latimes.com/politics/la-na-pol-donald-trump-immigration-speech-transcript-20160831-snap-htmlstory.html.

5 Catherine E. Shoichet, Susannah Cullinane, and Tal Kopan, "US Immigration: DACA and Dreamers Explained," CNN, September 5, 2017, http://www.cnn.com/2017/09/04/politics/daca-dreamers-immigration-program/index.html.

6 Muzaffar Chishti, Faye Hipsman, and Isabel Ball, "Fifty Years On, the 1965 Immigration and Nationality Act Continues to Reshape the United States," Migration Policy Institute, October 15, 2015, http://www.migrationpolicy.org/article/fifty-years-1965-immigration-and-nationality-act-continues-reshape-united-states.

7 Himilce Novas, *Everything You Need to Know about Latino History*, 2nd rev. ed. (New York, Penguin: 2003), 90.

8 Chishti et al., "Fifty Years On."

9 "StarPower—Use and Abuse of Power, Leadership, and Diversity," Simulation Training Systems, accessed July 30, 2017, http://www.simulationtrainingsystems.com/schools-and-charities/products/starpower/.

10 William H. Willimon, *Fear of the Other: No Fear in Love* (Nashville: Abingdon Press), 43.

6 Cough Syrup and Sandwiches

1 Carola Suârez-Orozco, Irina L. G. Todorova, and Josephine Louie, "Making Up for Lost Time: The Experience of Separation and Reunification among Immigrant Families," *Family Process* 41, no. 4 (December 2002): 625–43, http://onlinelibrary.wiley.com/doi/10.1111/j.1545-5300.2002.00625.x/abstract

2 Sonia Nazario, *Enrique's Journey: The Story of a Boy's Dangerous Odyssey to Reunite with His Mother* (New York: Random House, 2014).

3 *Strong's Exhaustive Concordance of the Bible*, Bible Hub, s.v. "5381. philoxenia," accessed July 23, 2017, http://biblehub.com/greek/5381.htm.

4 M. Daniel Carroll R., *Christians at the Border: Immigration, the Church, and the Bible* (Grand Rapids: Baker, 2008), 122.

5 "Why Should I Care?" G92, accessed July 24, 2017, http://g92.org/find-answers/why-should-i-care/.

7 Garment of Destiny

1 Stephen Goss, Alice Wade, J. Patrick Skirvin, Michael Morris, K. Mark Bye, and Danielle Huston, *Effects of Unauthorized Immigration on the Actuarial Status of the Social Security Trust Funds*, Actuarial Note no. 151 (Baltimore, MD: Social Security Administration, Office of the Chief Actuary, April 2013), 2, https://www.ssa.gov/oact/NOTES/pdf_notes/note151.pdf.

2 Bob Sullivan, "Courts: Using Another's SSN Not a Crime," NBC News, November 30, 2010, http://www.nbcnews.com/business/consumer/courts-using-anothers-ssn-not-crime-f6C10406382.

3 Eugene Volokh, "Using a False Social Security Number Is a Crime—but Is It a Crime 'of Moral Turpitude'?," *Washington Post*, August 26, 2016, https://www.washingtonpost.com/news/volokh-conspiracy/wp/2016/08/26/using-a-false-social-security-number-is-a-crime-but-is-it-a-crime-of-moral-turpitude/?utm_term=.c8cecf13b9d6.

4 Arias v. Lynch, 834 F.3d 823 (7th Cir. 2016) at 829.

5 Exec. Order. No. 13768, 82 Fed. Reg. 8799 (Jan. 25, 2017). The text of the order is available at https://www.whitehouse.gov/the

-press-òffice/2017/01/25/presidential-executive-order-enhancing -public-safety-interior-united.

6 Rudy Takala, "IRS Chief: Agency Encourages Illegal Immigrant Theft of SSNs to File Tax Returns," *Washington Examiner*, April 12, 2016, http://www.washingtonexaminer.com/agency-encourages -illegal-immigrant-theft-of-ssns-irs-chief/article/2588288.

7 Goss et al., *Effects of Unauthorized Immigration*.

8 Martin Luther King Jr., "Remaining Awake through a Great Revolution" (sermon, National Cathedral, Washington, DC, March 31, 1968).

9 In fact, immigration reform didn't come before Congress again until 2013. The Border Security, Economic Opportunity, and Immigration Modernization Act of 2013 was passed by the Senate in June 2013, but the U.S. House Speaker at the time, John Boehner, refused to introduce the bill on the House floor.

10 Martin Luther King Jr., *Letter from Birmingham City Jail*, April 16, 1963 (America Friends Service Committee, May 1963), 5, http://dp.la/item/f2f181011b1d780f5d6b74a36e533cdd.

11 William H. Willimon, *Fear of the Other: No Fear in Love* (Nashville: Abingdon Press, 2016), 39.

8 Mountains of Paperwork

1 American Immigration Council, *Fact Sheet: The Three- and Ten-Year Bars: How New Rules Expand Eligibility for Waivers*, October 28, 2016, https://www.americanimmigrationcouncil.org/research/ three-and-ten-year-bars.

2 Ibid.

3 Ibid.

4 Stephan Bauman, *Break Open the Sky: Saving Our Faith from a Culture of Fear* (New York: Multnomah, 2017), 3.

5 Ibid., 8–9.

9 Celebration

1 "U.S. Visa Fast Facts," CNN Library, last modified March 27, 2017, http://www.cnn.com/2017/03/23/us/us-visa-fast-facts/index.html.

2 "Visa Waiver Program," U.S. Department of State, accessed July 7, 2017, https://travel.state.gov/content/visas/en/visit/visa-waiver-program.html#reference.

3 "Ineligibilities and Waivers: Laws," U.S. Department of State, accessed July 7, 2017, https://travel.state.gov/content/visas/en/general/ineligibilities.html.

4 "Apply for a U.S. Visa in Guatemala," US Travel Docs, accessed July 7, 2017, http://www.ustraveldocs.com/gt/gt-niv-typeb1b2.asp.

5 John Ortberg, *The Life You've Always Wanted: Spiritual Disciplines for Ordinary People* (Grand Rapids: Zondervan, 1997), 72.

6 Ibid.

7 "What Is Wage Theft?," UCLA Labor Center, accessed July 8, 2017, https://www.labor.ucla.edu/wage-theft/.

8 Ruth Milkman, Ana Luz González, and Victor Narro with Annette Bernhardt, Nik Theodore, Douglas Heckathorn, Mirabai Auer, James DeFilippis, Jason Perelshteyn, Diana Polson, and Michael Spiller, *Wage Theft and Workplace Violations in Los Angeles: The Failure of Employment and Labor Law for Low-Wage Workers* (Institute for Research on Labor and Employment, University of California, Los Angeles, 2010), 53, https://www.labor.ucla.edu/downloads/wage-theft-and-workplace-violations-in-los-angeles-2/.

9 Brady Meixell and Ross Eisenbrey, *An Epidemic of Wage Theft Is Costing Workers Hundreds of Millions of Dollars a Year*, Economic Policy Institute, September 11, 2014, http://www.epi.org/publication/epidemic-wage-theft-costing-workers-hundreds/.

10 Ibid.

11 Eunice Hyunhye Cho, Tia Koonse, and Anthony Mischel, *Hollow Victories: The Crisis in Collecting Unpaid Wages for California's Workers* (National Employment Law Project and UCLA Labor Center, 2013), 2, https://www.labor.ucla.edu/downloads/hollow-victories-the-crisis-in-collecting-unpaid-wages-for-californias-workers-2/.

12 I am grateful to Leroy Barber, founder of the Voices Project, for introducing many of the ideas in this section to me.

10 Alien Relative

1 "Statue of Liberty," History, accessed July 15, 2017, http://www
.history.com/topics/statue-of-liberty.

2 "Chinese Immigration and the Chinese Exclusion Acts,"
U.S. Department of State Office of the Historian, accessed
July 15, 2017, https://history.state.gov/milestones/1866-1898/
chinese-immigration.

3 "Early American Immigration Policies," last modified
September 4, 2015, https://www.uscis.gov/history-and-genealogy/
our-history/agency-history/early-american-immigration-policies.

4 These are 2017 filing fees. I do not remember the exact amounts
for each form in 2007, probably because I was closing my eyes and
requesting cashier's checks. But I do recall the total at the time being
near $3,000, which does not seem implausible given current rates.

5 Joanna Dreby, *How Today's Immigration Enforcement Policies
Impact Children, Families, and Communities: A View from the
Ground* (Washington, DC: Center for American Progress, 2012), 1,
https://www.americanprogress.org/wp-content/uploads/2012/08/
DrebyImmigrationFamilies_execsumm.pdf.

6 Diane Guerrero, *In the Country We Love: My Family Divided* (New
York: Henry Holt, 2016), 83–88.

7 Heather Koball, Randy Capps, Sarah Hooker, Krista Perreira,
Andrea Campetella, Juan Manuel Pedroza, William Monson, and
Sandra Huerta, *Health and Social Service Needs of U.S.-Citizen
Children with Detained or Deported Immigrant Parents* (Washington,
DC: Urban Institute and Migration Policy Institute, 2015), http://
www.migrationpolicy.org/research/health-and-social
-service-needs-us-citizen-children-detained-or-deported-immigrant
-parents.

8 Manuel Pastor, "DAPA Matters," Center for American Progress,
November 19, 2015, https://www.americanprogress.org/issues/
immigration/reports/2015/11/19/125787/dapa-matters/.

9 Muzaffar Chishti and Faye Hipsman, "Supreme Court DAPA
Ruling a Blow to Obama Administration, Moves Immigration Back
to Political Realm," Migration Policy Institute, June 29, 2016, http://
www.migrationpolicy.org/article/supreme-court-dapa-ruling-blow
-obama-administration-moves-immigration-back-political-realm.

10 "Rescission of Memorandum Providing for Deferred Action for Parents of Americans and Lawful Permanent Residents ('DAPA'),'" Department of Homeland Security, June 15, 2017, https://www .dhs.gov/news/2017/06/15/rescission-memorandum-providing -deferred-action-parents-americans-and-lawful.

11 "The Religious Affiliation of U.S. Immigrants: Majority Christian, Rising Share of Other Faiths," Pew Research Center, May 17, 2013, http://www.pewforum.org/2013/05/17/the-religious-affiliation-of-us -immigrants/.

11 Hiding in Plain Sight

1 John Morton, director, U.S. Immigration and Customs Enforcement, memorandum, "Enforcements Actions at or Focused on Sensitive Locations," October 24, 2011, policy no. 0029.2, FEA no. 30-112-002b, https://www.ice.gov/doclib/ero-outreach/ pdf/10029.2-policy.pdf.

2 Alexia Salvatierra, interview with the author, March 7, 2017.

3 "Cities of Refuge," *The NIV Study Bible* (Grand Rapids, MI: Zondervan, 1995), 237.

4 Salvatierra, interview.

5 Judith McDaniel, "The Sanctuary Movement, Then and Now," *Religion and Politics*, February 21, 2017, http://religionandpolitics .org/2017/02/21/the-sanctuary-movement-then-and-now/.

6 Ibid.

7 Ibid.

8 Ibid.

9 For more on the ministry of El Refugio, visit http:// elrefugiostewart.org/.

10 Marie Friedmann Marquardt, "Brother of Killed Asylum Seeker: 'Tell the Judge He Told the Truth,'" *Religion News Service*, March 9, 2017, http://religionnews.com/2017/03/09/ brother-of-killed-asylum-seeker-tell-the-judge-he-told-the-truth/.

11 This and the information in the next two paragraphs is from Salvatierra, interview.

12 Fences and Walls

1 Our experience took place in 2008 before passports were required to visit Mexico. I expect entry methods have changed since the visit described here.

2 President Donald Trump News and Live Speech 2017, "Donald Trump First AD Commercial TV AD Campaign," posted January 4, 2016, YouTube video, 0:31, https://www.youtube.com/watch?v=AEAJrT8PeOo.

3 Carolyn Edds, "Donald Trump's First TV Ad Shows Migrants 'At the Southern Border,' but They're Actually in Morocco," PolitiFact, January 4, 2016, http://www.politifact.com/truth-o-meter/statements/2016/jan/04/donald-trump/donald-trumps-first-tv-ad-shows-migrants-southern-/.

4 "An Up-Close Look at U.S./Mexico Border Where Trump Proposes to Build Wall," CBS Los Angeles, February 20, 2017, http://losangeles.cbslocal.com/2017/02/20/an-up-close-look-at-u-s-mexico-border-where-trump-proposes-to-build-wall/.

5 Leslie Berestein, "Highway Safety Sign Becomes Running Story on Immigration," *San Diego Union-Tribune*, April 10, 2005, http://legacy.sandiegouniontribune.com/uniontrib/20050410/news_1n10signs.html.

6 George Sandeman, "Make Art, Not Wall: Artists Use Colourful Murals to Decorate US-Mexico Border Wall and Clever Tricks to Make It 'Disappear,'" January 29, 2017, https://www.thesun.co.uk/news/2733997/artists-use-colourful-murals-to-decorate-us-mexico-border-wall-and-clever-tricks-to-make-it-disappear/.

7 The Editorial Board, "A Chance to Reset the Republican Race," *New York Times*, January 30, 2016, https://www.nytimes.com/2016/01/31/opinion/sunday/a-chance-to-reset-the-republican-race.html.

8 "U.S. Spends More on Immigration Enforcement than on FBI, DEA, Secret Service and All Other Federal Criminal Law Enforcement Agencies Combined," Migration Policy Institute, January 7, 2013, http://www.migrationpolicy.org/news/us-spends-more-immigration-enforcement-fbi-dea-secret-service-all-other-federal-criminal-law.

9 Daniel González, "How Many Mexicans Actually Cross the Border Illegally?" *Arizona Republic* (Phoenix), October 9, 2016, http://www.azcentral.com/story/news/politics/border-issues/2016/

10/09/how-many-mexicans-actually-cross-border-illegally/
91280026/.

10 Ibid.

11 Find out more about Friendship Park at friendshippark.org/
home.

12   Yanan Wang, "At One Border Park, Separated Immigrant
Families Hug across a Steel Divide," *Washington Post*, May 1, 2016,
https://www.washingtonpost.com/national/for-families-divided-by
-a-mesh-fence-a-rare-chance-to-embrace/2016/05/01/d0fdcf08-0b07
-11e6-a6b6-2e6de3695b0e_story.html?utm_term=.98a01108abd8.

13 "How Trump's Wall Compares to Other Famous Walls,"
BBC News, January 25, 2017, http://www.bbc.co.uk/newsbeat/
article/38743252/how-trumps-wall-compares-to-other
-famous-walls.

13 Bed Quota

1 Martin Luther King Jr., "Remaining Awake through a Great
Revolution" (sermon, National Cathedral, Washington, DC, March
31, 1968).

2 "Stewart Detention Center," CCA, accessed July 29, 2017, http://
www.cca.com/facilities/stewart-detention-center.

3 "Immigrant Detainees in Georgia More Likely to Be Deported
Than Detainees Elsewhere," Southern Poverty Law Center,
August 23, 2016, https://www.splcenter.org/news/2016/08/23/
immigrant-detainees-georgia-more-likely-be-deported-detainees
-elsewhere.

4 "Phasing Out Our Use of Private Prisons," U.S. Department of
Justice (archives), August 18, 2016, accessed July 29, 2017, https://
www.justice.gov/archives/opa/blog/phasing-out-our-use-private
-prisons.

5 Robert Costa, Sari Horwitz, and Matt Zapotosky, "Jeff Sessions
Says He Plans to Stay in Role, Despite Trump's Comments about
Him," *Washington Post*, July 20, 2017, https://www
.washingtonpost.com/world/national-security/attorney-general
-jeff-sessions-says-he-plans-to-stay-in-role-despite-trumps
-comments-about-him/2017/07/20/527e53d4-6d51-11e7-9c15
-177740635e83_story.html?utm_term=.db716fd1fe99.

6 Steven Nelson, "Private Prison Companies, Punched in the Gut, Will Keep Most Federal Business," *U.S. News and World Report,* August 18, 2016, https://www.usnews.com/news/articles/2016-08 -18/private-prison-companies-punched-in-the-gut-will-keep-most -federal-business.

7 Mary Small, Dawy Rkasnuam, and Silky Shah, *A Toxic Relationship: Private Prisons and U.S. Immigration Detention* (Washington, DC: Detention Watch Network, 2016), https:// www.detentionwatchnetwork.org/sites/default/files/reports/A%20 Toxic%20Relationship_DWN.pdf.

8 "Detention Quotas," Detention Watch Network, accessed July 29, 2017, https://www.detentionwatchnetwork.org/issues/ detention-quotas.

9 "Immigration Detention Fact Sheet" (New York, NY: Human Rights First, 2013), https://www.humanrightsfirst.org/uploads/pdfs/ immigration-detention-fact-sheet-jan-2013.pdf.

10 Jerry Markon, "Can a 3-Year Old Represent Herself in Immigration Court? This Judge Things So," *Washington Post,* March 5, 2016, https://www.washingtonpost.com/world/national -security/can-a-3-year-old-represent-herself-in-immigration -court-this-judge-thinks-so/2016/03/03/5be59a32-db25-11e5-925f -1d10062cc82d_story.html?utm_term=.af5965df3daa.

14 Citizenship without Borders

1 Paul Taylor, Ana Gonzalez-Barrera, Jeffrey S. Passel, and Mark Hugo Lopez, "An Awakened Giant: The Hispanic Electorate Is Likely to Double by 2030," Pew Research Center, November 14, 2012, http://www.pewhispanic.org/2012/11/14/an-awakened-giant -the-hispanic-electorate-is-likely-to-double-by-2030/.

2 Hansi Lo Wang, "Green Card Holders Worry about Trump's Efforts to Curtail Immigration," NPR's *Morning Edition,* February 21, 2017, http://www.npr.org/2017/02/21/516375460/green-card -holders-worry-about-trump-s-efforts-to-curtain-immigration.

3 Ibid.

4 Expatriation Act of 1907, Pub. L. No. 193, 34 Stat. 2534 § 3 (1907).

5 Candice Lewis Bredbenner, *A Nationality of Her Own: Women, Marriage, and the Law of Citizenship* (Berkeley: University of California Press, 1998), 6.

6 Mackenzie v. Hare 239 U.S. 299 (2015) at 79.

7 Tanya Ballard Brown, "That Time American Women Lost Their Citizenship Because They Married Foreigners," NPR's *Codeswitch*, March 17, 2017, http://www.npr.org/sections/codeswitch/2017/03/17/520517665/that-time-american-women-lost-their-citizenship-because-they-married-foreigners.

8 For more information on the 2017 RAISE Act, see Peter Baker, "Trump Supports Plan to Cut Legal Immigration by Half," *New York Times*, August 2, 2017, https://www.nytimes.com/2017/08/02/us/politics/trump-immigration.html?mcubz=1.

9 Find out more about Bridge at www.bridge-guatemala.com.

THE AUTHOR

Sarah Quezada is a writer and non-profit professional in Atlanta, Georgia. She has a master's in sociology from the University of Kentucky, and her writing has been published in *Christianity Today*, *Relevant*, *Sojourners*, and InTouch Ministries, among others. She has worked with Azusa Pacific University and Mission Year, and was selected for an Emerging Leaders Cohort of the Christian Community Development Association. She and her husband, Billy, serve at their church, facilitating visits to immigrant detainees at Stewart Detention Center in partnership with El Refugio Ministry. They are the parents of two children. To connect with Sarah, visit her website www.sarahquezada .com or find her on Facebook (fb.me/SarahDQuezada), Twitter (@SarahQuezada), or Instagram (@SarahQuezada).